THE BLACKHALL GUIDE TO EMPLC

developing people to develop your company

About the Author

Philip Cripps is Chief Executive of Thameside International, one of the UK's leading personnel development consultancies. He has lectured throughout the world and written many articles for leading business magazines on management, negotiation, sales and human resource development.

THE BLACKHALL GUIDE TO EMPLOYEE DEVELOPMENT

developing people to develop your company

PHILIP C CRIPPS

This book was typeset by Gough Typesetting Services for
Blackhall Publishing
8 Priory Hall, Stillorgan
Co. Dublin
Ireland

e-mail: blackhall@eircom.net
www.blackhallpublishing.com

ISBN: 1 842180 02 9

A catalogue record for this book is
available from the British Library.

Printed in Ireland by
Johnswood Press

TABLE OF CONTENTS

APPENDICES

Appendix – One to Six

Checklists – One to Fifteen

INTRODUCTION

Thank you for choosing to read *The Blackhall Guide to Employee Development: Developing People to Develop your Company*. By the way, why did you make the decision? I have no doubt that some of the influencing factors included your desire to grow your business, to achieve greater successes and to make more money. Achieving these goals is dependent upon a variety of factors and high on the list is that of EMPLOYEE COMPETENCE. After all a company is only as good as the people it employs.

So people should be every employer's biggest asset. However, they can also be an employer's biggest liability. How can you ensure that people become an asset rather than a liability? Whilst not disregarding such issues as remuneration levels and working conditions, the most important determinant of whether employees become and remain assets of a company is MANAGEMENT ACTION. If a manager is committed to the development of his or her people then companies grow and prosper.

The aim of this book is to expand your appreciation of the nature and scope of your personnel development responsibilities, influence your attitudes towards these responsibilities, introduce you to new employee development techniques and explain how you can enhance your skills to enable you to "develop your people to develop your company".

Part One

RESPONSIBILITIES, PRINCIPLES AND GUIDELINES

CHAPTER 1

DO YOU RECOGNISE THE SCOPE OF YOUR TRAINING RESPONSIBILITIES?

When I was appointed to my first line management role I was told that one of my most important responsibilities was to train and develop my team members. But sadly that pronouncement was not enlarged upon in a way that enabled me to understand the nature and scope of my training responsibilities, or the distinction between training and developing people. The scope of responsibility within the area was very wide, it then became clear that training and development are not the same thing. Training is the imparting of new knowledge to an individual or group. Development occurs when you are seeking to enhance peoples' existing skills.

For today's manager his or her training and development responsibilities can be divided into two categories:

The first is GROUP TRAINING: this can include running business meetings, giving formal presentations, chairing discussion sessions and leading and participating in group role play exercises.

The second is INDIVIDUAL TRAINING: this can include on-the-job training, delegation, counselling, job rotation, job secondment, project work and even corrective and disciplinary discussions.

You combine the tasks of knowledge conveyor or skills developer, advisor, counsellor, motivator and attitude influencer. You should exercise *"Management by Suggestion"* rather than *"Management by Directive"*. You help people to recognise their strengths and shortcomings. The diversity of these responsibilities can concern or even frighten a newly appointed manager. Questions arise in the manager's mind, such as:

How do I plan the training?

How do I fit it in with all my other responsibilities?

How much time should I devote to training activities?

What skills do I need to master?

Will my staff accept me as their trainer?

Will I enjoy training people?

How can I measure the results I achieve?

Let's start to answer the questions shown on the previous page and many more by reviewing some of the most important principles and guidelines you should adopt when training your team members.

CHAPTER 2

HOW TO GENERATE THE RIGHT FRAME OF MIND TOWARDS YOUR TRAINING RESPONSIBILITIES

Common statements made by newly appointed managers include:

Developing people is easy – it's just a matter of telling them what to do

and

Training is just a matter of common sense

and

If you push people hard enough they improve

Within a very short space of time these managers are going to discover that developing people is far from easy. It is a complex activity and one that generates enormous satisfaction and tremendous frustration – often in equal amounts!

Developing people involves the following:

Persuading people to want to do what you want them to do

and

Helping people to achieve what they want

The starting point for every manager who WANTS to succeed as a developer of people, is the acquisition and maintenance of a series of ATTITUDES, including:

1. BEING INTERESTED IN PEOPLE

If you are only interested in yourself then you will never generate AIDA with your staff. AIDA has often been described as the oldest sales acronym. It was created in the 1920s and refers to:

Securing someone's .... **A**ttention
Creating .... **I**nterest
Stimulating .... **D**esire
and prompting.. **A**ction

Successful developers of people all derive enormous satisfaction from seeing individuals grow.

2. BELIEVING IN YOUR OWN ABILITY

The diverse nature of your training responsibilities and the skills associated with the fulfilment of these tasks can give some managers cause for concern. Those concerns are often aggravated by two unhelpful people – I am referring to SID and TOM. SID, or to give him his full name, SELF IMPOSED DOUBT is the little voice inside you that tells you how unsuccessful you will be if you embark upon something new, different and difficult.

Do not listen to SID or his companion TOM. TOM is THE OUTSIDE MESSENGER. It never ceases to amaze me how often people who purport to be our friends or colleagues try to put us off a particular course of action. Do you recall the last time someone said to you such things as:

You can't be serious about doing......

You're not going to try that are you?

You're never going to attempt that?

Do they really believe they are being helpful? Ignore the TOMs of the world, believe in your own ability and become a conscious optimist.

CHAPTER 3

WHAT ARE THE MOST IMPORTANT PRINCIPLES AND GUIDELINES YOU SHOULD ADOPT AND FOLLOW WHEN FULFILLING YOUR RESPONSIBILITIES TO TRAIN AND DEVELOP YOUR TEAM MEMBERS?

1. Training and development is a process of realising the potential of individuals.

   As managers we can and should act as the catalyst for the release of our team members' potential.

   If your company is to grow you have to find ways of realising the potential within each of your staff.

   How is this achieved?

   Successful managers resemble intrepid drillers of oil. Oil companies look for the right geological conditions, where the potential for oil is greatest. Managers look within their companies for people with the potential to grow. However, even when the oil companies find what appear to be the right conditions the only thing they extract is mud or dust. When you train people who appear to have the right potential you can also experience disappointment as that apparent potential is not realised. But the oil companies keep drilling and you must keep training your staff – otherwise you'll never strike the equivalent of the oilmen's black gold.

2. Training should be designed to harness the natural personality of an individual.

   Your team is likely to comprise individuals with widely differing personalities and that can often be one of the team's key strengths. You have to work with individual personalities since they cannot be changed.

3. You should NOT try to produce employees who are copies of yourself. Uniformity may create harmony but it does little for initiative and imagination. Allow individuals to flex their intellectual muscles and to bring their thoughts and ideas to the fore.

4. You should SELL and not TELL staff your ideas.

   The act of telling someone to do something is an easy one. It needs little, if any, preparatory thought and can be completed quickly. However, ask yourself if you like to be told what to do. This book will show you how to "sell" ideas to your staff.

   If you want to develop the confidence and competence of your staff then they need to believe in what you are saying and recognise the benefits they can obtain from adopting your ideas and suggestions. Therefore, you have to use persuasive and consultative communication techniques. Your aim must be to *"elevate people"* – that is to say, to make them feel needed, important, respected and of value.

5. You need to develop a PASSIVE QUESTIONING MANNER.

   We will cover the power of structured questioning at a later stage (in Part Four). However, at this point I want to highlight the importance of asking questions in a passive manner. The term "*passive*", in the context of questioning, refers to the act of asking a question without visually or verbally indicating your attitude towards the subject within the question.

   Far too many of us pose questions in a manner which encourages the recipient of the question to respond to our expression of attitude and not to the content of our question. You have to work hard to master the skills of passive questioning. However, as you will discover, the results of your efforts can be very positive.

6. You must set the HIGHEST PERSONAL STANDARDS.

   The American expression *"Walk the talk"* comes readily to mind when I reflect on the principle above. People will never respond to your training and development activities unless you demonstrate that your standards are always high.

   The standards to which I am referring include:
   - Consistency of application. You cannot expect people to apply knowledge and skills if your use of either or both is irregular.
   - Planning and preparation. All managerial action should start with planning. If you demonstrate that you plan your business activities then your team members will be encouraged to plan theirs.

7. Practice LISTENING TO YOUR STAFF.

   In Part Four I outline the differences between hearing and listening. I also describe how to become an active listener.

   Your staff expect to hear from you – but they also expect you to listen to their ideas. Successful developers of staff know that, ironically, the more they listen the more they learn.

8. Training is about INFORMING FIRST AND PERFORMING SECOND.

   Regrettably many trainers, especially those who are employed in full time training roles, concentrate more on how they present their subject matter rather than the content of their material.

   It is a question of balance. But if you have tipped the scales too far in the direction of presentation always tip them back in the direction of content.

9. Training consists primarily of changing ATTITUDES.

   Improving peoples' performance almost always starts with the issue of attitude – an individual's frame of mind. Behaviour is the physical manifestation of attitude.

   If employees' attitudes are receptive and positive then they will be willing to accept new knowledge, to develop existing skills and acquire new skills. You have the opportunity and responsibility to shape your team's attitudes. Throughout your managerial career you will find that the task of influencing individuals' attitudes will be your most important.

10. Stimulate HEALTHY COMPETITION amongst your staff.

    Competition helps to bring out the best in most people – provided it is not divisive in nature. When you consider creating competitive situations within your team ask yourself these questions:

    > *Will EVERY member of the team respond positively to the competitive situation?*
    >
    > *Will the competition UNIFY the team or create factions?*
    >
    > *Will the competition have a short-term positive effect but a long-term negative result?*

    I appreciate that your answers to each question must be subjective ones. None the less it is important for you to consider each question before you take any actions.

11. Retain CONTROL OF YOUR EMOTIONS regardless of the training situation.

    The training and development of employees can be and often is, a frustrating process. However, if you allow your frustrations to surface each time one of your staff fails to do, or achieve, that which you were training him or her to do, then you will dent, and possibly destroy, the confidence of that person.

12. Be AN INITIATOR OF IDEAS – but don't spoon feed.

    It is easy for a manager to fall into the trap of thinking that the development of his team members depends upon him being the fountain of all knowledge. Of course you have a responsibility to introduce your team to new ideas, but letting your staff discover their own answers on occasions is a development technique and not abdication on your part.

13. Be DEPENDABLE – don't let your team members down when it comes to giving them time.

    Almost every manager I have ever met has complained at some time about either, *"not having enough time"* or, *"having to cancel training sessions with team members"*.

    If you promise to spend a certain amount of time with your staff, stick to your promise. Yes, there are always distractions, interruptions and demands from other people. When these occur remember one important fact:

    > *The training and development of your team members is your most important task*

    By the way, you may have to diplomatically remind your boss about this fact from time to time.

14. Show genuine enthusiasm when you train – SMILE! – with your eyes as well as your mouth.

    How can any member of your team become enthused about developing him or herself if he is faced with a boss who lacks enthusiasm. Reflect on my saying:

    > *If you feel happy why not notify your face*

15. Consider your team members as PEOPLE FIRST AND EMPLOYEES SECOND.

    The more interest you show in your staff the better you will understand each person. The better you understand each person the more likely you will be to motivate rather than demotivate that person.

16. REMAIN A REALIST when you train and seek to develop your staff.

    Be realistic about each person's potential and your ability to develop that individual. As managers we would all like to have a team that is comprised of *"sure-fire winners"*. However, the vast majority of us manage a group of individuals with mixed attitudes and abilities, regardless of our efforts to identify and recruit the very best. As a result realism must be applied to our assessment of how far we can develop individuals.

17. APPRAISE REGULARLY the ways in which you train and develop your team members.

    You need to ensure your training remains fresh. If it becomes repetitive in content, presentation or format then it will not inspire and motivate individuals. Keep yourself aware of new training ideas and methods by reading newspapers, magazines, journals and by attending training events.

18. Delete the word *"PROBLEM"* from your vocabulary.

    Management brings you face to face with problems every day. However, it is your attitude that determines how you address each problem. Your challenge is to show your staff that the difficulties they face can only be resolved by POSITIVE ACTIONS. When conveying this fact delete the word *"problem"* from your vocabulary. Problem is a word that stimulates negative thoughts in the majority of people. Have you ever heard anybody express such statements as:

    We've got a problem

    or

    Yet another problem has arisen

    . . . . with a smile on their face?

    Substitute the words *"issue"*, *"topic"*, *"subject"* or *"matter"* for the word *"problem"*. These words confirm that there is something to be addressed, but they can be expressed in a far more positive way, for example:

    That's an important issue, let's look for a solution

    or

    That matter needs addressing. How should we tackle it?

19. You need to TRUST your people.

    Employing staff is a potentially risky business – but it is a measurable risk. Your team have to recognise that you support the saying *"trust is a must"*. However, that trust isn't blind. You need to monitor people's behaviour and performance, but in a low key way. Only when your trust is abused are counselling or corrective discussions necessary. Each of these important activities is reviewed later in the book.

20. Do not show your FEARS, ANXIETIES and CONCERNS to your people.

    It has often been said that enthusiasm is infectious – well the lack of it is far more infectious. If you reveal your concerns to your staff through your lack of enthusiasm then their desire to follow your suggestions, adopt your ideas and implement your training will be diminished.

CHAPTER 4

DO YOU REALLY ENJOY TRAINING AND DEVELOPING PEOPLE?

Before you respond to my question with a resounding "yes" I would like you to consider your answer very carefully. Training and developing people does not just represent a commitment in time and money – it is an emotional commitment. You have to derive a real and sustained enjoyment from helping people to grow and realise their potential.

For many managers that enjoyment is compromised by a variety of factors. These include:

1. Employees' negative reactions to training.

   It is strange that so many people consider that training is initiated for negative rather than positive reasons. In other words training takes place only when something has gone wrong. It is also ironic that when most potential employees are being interviewed for a new job they ask about the training they will receive. Does something strange happen to these people when they join their new employer? Does their desire for training simply vanish? And what makes them become defensive about their need for training?

2. Some employees' unwillingness (and not inability) to put the training they receive into practice.

   It is frustrating to spend time training someone only to find that the individual does not put his or her new found knowledge into practice. You ask yourself the *"Why?"* question and rarely provide yourself with a satisfactory answer.

3. Some employees treat training as an unnecessary distraction from their normal day to day work. I have often heard employees say such things as:

   I'd love to go on that course – but I just don't have the time.

   and

   Yes, it would be nice if you could spend a couple of hours helping me with my formal presentation technique – but you know the work load I've got at present – so can we schedule something for next month?

This book will help you to evaluate your attitude towards and aptitude for developing people. I would also like it to stimulate your desire to fulfil your most important responsibility as a line manager – that of developing your staff.

Part Two

CREATING THE RIGHT ENVIRONMENT FOR DEVELOPING YOUR PEOPLE

CHAPTER 5

IS TRAINING AND DEVELOPMENT A COST TO YOUR BUSINESS OR AN INVESTMENT IN IT?

When economic times get tough what is one of the first areas of expenditure to get cut in most companies? Yes, training. But why?

I don't think the answer is hard to find. Many companies hold the view that training is difficult to measure in terms of its effectiveness and, therefore, the situation justifies cutting (and sometimes eliminating) expenditure in this area.

But if companies continue to take this easy option the long-term consequences could be dire. For if your people stop growing so will your company.

The challenge lies in planning, organising and conducting training that impacts directly on the company's bottom line.

How can this challenge be met?

I would like to ask you ten questions about the ways in which you have conducted training and development activities within your company. If you can respond *"yes"* to each question then your expenditure is already producing qualitative and quantitative results. It is an investment. If you reply *"no"* to more than four of my questions don't take out the financial scalpel and cut your training budget. Reassess your approach to developing your people.

Here are my ten questions:

1. *Is all of the training and development undertaken within your company conducted after a detailed assessment has been completed to determine if there is a real need for the activity?*

Too much training is undertaken for the wrong purposes. For example, I know of companies who initiate training for their staff as a reward for employees long service, or for working exceptionally long hours, or for spending many nights away from their families. If you want to reward people please do – but use means other than training.

I also know employers whose motivations for training people include the following:

Well John hasn't been on any courses recently

or

It's Steve's turn to go on a course

or

> *We had better send a few people off for some training – or we'll lose our budget next year*

If you cannot justify the need for training don't do it.

2. *Do you always establish qualitative or quantitative objectives for the training you initiate within your organisation?*

When people complain to me that it is hard to measure the results of training my initial response is always the same. I ask the question … *"WHAT RESULTS DO YOU WANT TO ACHIEVE?"*

The question always stimulates lots of discussion because the respondent, often for the first time, recognises that he or she has not given the subject of results or outcome sufficient thought. Until you know what you want to achieve from your training how can you establish meaningful measurements?

I want to distinguish at this point between the terms *"qualitative"* and *"quantitative"* results.

A quantifiable result is NUMERICAL in nature. For example, by introducing a factory worker to new working methods he could increase his productivity from twelve units an hour to twenty.

Whenever you seek to establish the results you want to achieve from your investment in training focus first on quantifiable outcomes. They provide you with clear cut measurements which all staff understand.

Whilst it would be ideal if the outcomes of all training and development activities could be measured quantifiably this will never be the case in practise.

A great deal of training is aimed at the achievement of qualitative improvements in peoples' performance. And there are more difficulties associated with the establishment of qualitative measurements than there are for quantitative.

Your starting point is to ask yourself the question:

How do I want the person to work as a result of the training?

You are considering such issues as attitudinal and behavioural changes. But ultimately you are seeking to determine what these changes will produce in terms of outcome. You must be specific in terms of the results you want to achieve.

Here are a few examples of specific qualitative measurements for a training session on counselling and corrective interviewing.

"As a result of providing Ann with training in counselling and corrective techniques I want her to achieve the following:

— *to plan each counselling and corrective interview in accordance with the twelve stage approach outlined during the training.*

— *to demonstrate empathy with her team members during counselling and corrective interviews.*

— *to always use structured questions to identify individuals attitudes, motivations, opinions, views and concerns.*

— *to conclude each counselling and corrective interview with a series of written action agreements."*

Far too many directors, managers and owners of businesses NEVER determine the outcome they desire from training and developing their people, and those that do express vague or unspecific goals. For example:

I want Jill to demonstrate a better attitude

I'd like David to be more assertive as a result of the training

If Brian is more confident as a result of the training I'll be happy

Take the time to establish clear and concise objectives. Remind yourself of the saying. . . . *"If it can't be measured it isn't an improvement"*.

For examples of other quantifiable and qualitative training objectives refer to Checklist one and two on pages 159 and 160.

3. *Has the person selected to undertake the training been trained to train?*

It is one thing to know the subject matter you want to present to the person or persons you need to train or develop. It is quite another to know HOW to present it. Most of us are familiar with the training technique of *"Sitting next to Nellie"*. The expression refers to assigning a new employee to a long serving employee for training. Nellie may very well know the subject, but she also knows the shortcuts and she may well convey as many bad habits as good to her unsuspecting trainee. I will be covering the subject of training skills later in the book.

4. *Does the RIGHT person always undertake the training and development activities?*

When you manage a team of people it is your responsibility to train and develop each person. However, that does not mean you are always the right person to fulfil the training. Always consider whether there is someone in your company or externally that could undertake the activity more effectively than you. Some managers consider a decision to assign the responsibility for some aspects of training to another person as an abdication. It is not. It is simply making the best use of available resources.

5. *Do you budget sufficient time for the development of your people?*

When you are planning your business activities, and entering them into your diary, do you always budget specific times for the development of your people? Is that time sufficient? Or is it squeezed into your busy schedule and invariably squeezed out by events.

Now I recognise that there may be some readers of this book who are thinking, *"Do I really need to spend so much time and effort developing my people?"*

The question may have been prompted by a variety of issues, such as:

No one ever developed me and I've done all right

I'm good at my job, so why can't everyone else be?

Well before you consider your competence and indispensability as reasons for abdicating your personnel development responsibilities read this poem:

Sometime when you're feeling important
Sometime when your ego's in bloom,
Sometime when you take it for granted,
You're the best qualified guy in the room,
Sometime when you feel that your going
Would leave an unfillable hole,
Just follow these simple instructions
and see how they humble your soul!

Take a bucket and fill it up with water,
Put your hand in it up to your wrist,
Pull it out – and the hole that remains
Is the measure of how you'll be missed.

The moral of this is quite simple;
Do always the best that you can.
Be proud of yourself – but remember –
There is no indispensable man.

Make time for your team members and protect that time from those who would like to steal it.

6. *Does all of the training you undertake relate directly to your company's business objectives?*

Over the last 30 years numerous training initiatives have been launched within business circles which could, at best, be described as *"the flavour of the month"*. These vogue ideas have attracted attention and have earned some training providers a healthy (if short term) living. Sadly many of the initiatives have fallen into the categories of *"esoteric"*, *"academic"* or *"the emperor's new clothes"*. Money has been expended by companies – no return has been secured – cynicism has been generated – future training budgets have been compromised.

Ensure your training and development investment relates directly to the goals your company or organisation has committed itself to achieve.

7. *Do all the training and development activities you undertake conclude with participants committing themselves in WRITING to the achievement of quantitative and/or qualitative goals?*

Far too many formal or on-the-job training events end with managers expressing such things as:

> *Well I hope you have enjoyed the course and will want to put things into practice.*
>
> *We've had three busy days together and covered a great many subjects which I am sure you will want to master.*
>
> *Its been good working with you this afternoon and I'm sure you've learned a lot.*

Hope may spring eternal – but as managers we cannot rely on a hope that the people we seek to develop will respond to our guidance. The achievement of measurable results is far easier to ensure if each recipient of training completes a PERSONAL ACTION PLAN (see the appendix section of the book).

The Action Plan requires the employee to define WHAT he or she will do as a result of the training, HOW the commitment will be fulfilled, by WHEN the objectives will be achieved, or when actions will commence, and what is expected to RESULT from the actions.

Most of us have made new year resolutions at some time in our life. But how many of us have committed these to paper? The act of committing goals to paper is highly significant. It forces us to face up to the issue of ACCOUNTABILITY. When goals are recorded on paper far more are achieved than those which were only expressed as verbal intentions.

For examples of ACTION PLAN documents refer to Appendix one and two on pages 147 and 148.

8. *Is training and development ongoing within your Company or Organisation?*

Training and development is not something that happens when the mood takes a manager or when his conscience is pricked by one of his team members. It has to be continuous and ongoing.

Successful managers prepare a training plan for each member of their team. The plan is drawn up following detailed discussions with each team member and should incorporate, as a minimum, the following:

- The training OBJECTIVES (The results to be achieved)
- The training METHODS (How the training will be delivered)
- The TIME to be allocated for the training
- The DATE(s) allocated for the training
- WHO is to undertake the training
- WHERE the training is to take place (On the job? Off the job? Location?)

The time period covered by the plan can vary considerably depending on the circumstances. However, once the plan is put in place it should be ongoing and the results recorded within a training record system. Such a system could be computer and/or paper based. The records should be maintained throughout an employee's time with the company.

For an example of a TRAINING AND DEVELOPMENT PLAN refer to Appendix three on page 149.

9. *Is every director and manager within your company or organisation COMMITTED to developing employees?*

Many years ago I worked for a Canadian entrepreneur who built a highly successful multinational company. He was both a complex and interesting man and a person from whom I learned a great deal. One of the lessons I learned resulted from me asking him a question about his total commitment to training staff. I asked him why he spent so much money training staff who subsequently left the Company to join other organisations. His reply was in two parts.

He acknowledged that employees did leave the Company. But he maintained that if he did not train staff they would leave even sooner and it would be more difficult to attract new personnel.

The second part of his reply could be summarised as follows:

If you think training is expensive, try calculating the cost of ignorance

Throughout the six years that I worked for his company I benefited from thousands of pounds of investment in my development. I grew and so did the results I achieved. I wanted to provide my boss with a payback. He paid the training bill but I was the one feeling I owed something.

Each of us as directors, managers or owners of our business needs to recognise that there is a real cost to not developing our staff.

We need to create an environment for learning which encourages as many staff as possible to realise their potential. You know financiers often refer to ROI, by which they mean Return on Investment. I also like to refer to ROI – only I am talking about Return on Involvement.

10. *Is all of the training you undertake (or is undertaken by your managerial colleagues) PLANNED IN DETAIL?*

You cannot reply *"yes"* if you do not:

— define the objectives for the training

— calculate the time needed for the training

— assess, and prepare for, the attitudinal reactions of your staff to the subjects you wish to cover

— select the most suitable location for the training

— prepare your *"opening"* to the session

— support your training with appropriate visual aids

— prepare handouts/training materials where necessary

When managers action each of the questions I have raised then the full chain of training events and effects in a company can be expressed as follows:

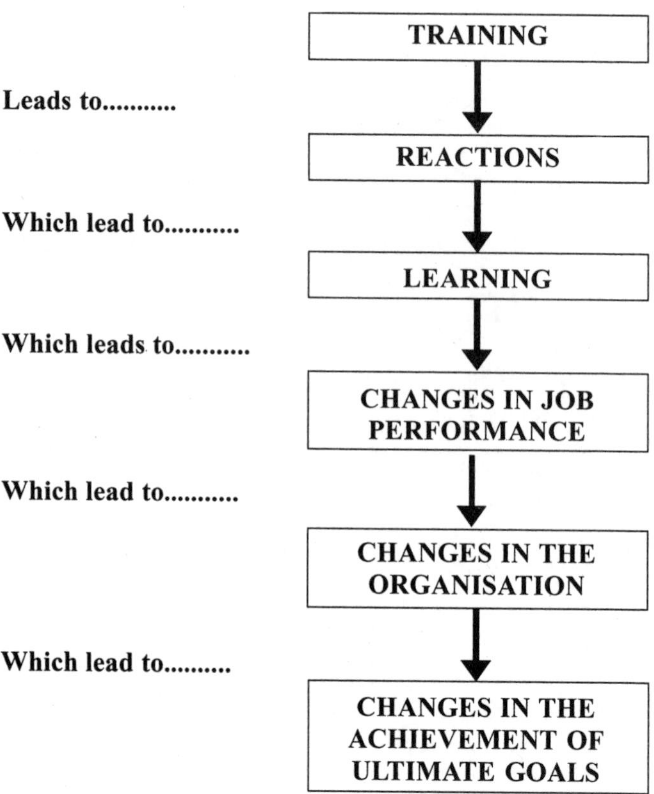

Part Three

YOU AS A DEVELOPER OF PEOPLE

CHAPTER 6

DEVELOPING YOUR PEOPLE MEANS GIVING LEADERSHIP

Successful people managers have strong leadership qualities and, I am sure, would agree with the quote attributed to Lao Tzu, a Chinese philosopher who died over 2000 years ago:

> *As for the best leaders, the people do not notice*
> *The next best, the people honour and praise*
> *The next, the people fear*
> *And the next, the people hate*
> *And when the best leader's work is done, the people say...*
> *We did it ourselves*

Successful leaders can not be typecast. However, they all demonstrate a number of common qualities, including:

— decisiveness

— credibility

— natural charisma

— responsibility – accountability

— initiative – creativity

— focus

— vision

— direction

— trust

— fairness

— communication skills

— motivation skills

— integrity

— strong personality

— courage

Successful managers recognise that leadership does not equate with popularity. It is concerned with RESULTS and RESPONSIBILITY.

Leaders focus upon individuals performance, standards and values. They are not concerned with personalities.

Leaders are individuals who attract better people than themselves into their service.

Study Checklist fifteen on page 185 to assess your leadership qualities.

Chapter 7

HOW TO UNDERSTAND YOUR TEAM MEMBERS

Recognising that, as a people manager, you have the responsibility to develop the people who work with and for you is one thing. Knowing how to fulfil that responsibility is quite another. Where do you start?

Those of us who have had to answer the question for ourselves, because we were not trained to train before we took on our role, soon discovered that there are an enormous number of traps into which you can fall.

If you are yet to take on a people management role, I would like to show you how to avoid many of the most common traps. If you have fulfilled a people management role for many years I would like to introduce you to what I am sure will be a new and exciting approach to identifying the training and development needs of your team members.

There is a natural inclination amongst managers to approach the identification of their team members' training and development needs by asking in which area the person in question needs to improve his or her performance.

This approach focuses exclusively on what the company wants from the individual. But what does the individual want for him or herself? A successful manager recognises that he has to develop his or her staff to achieve the company's objectives while seeking to satisfy (in part, if not whole) the personal ambitions or aspirations of each team member. This obligates the manager to identify some very important information about each member of staff, including:

— What are the ambitions or aspirations of each of my team members?

— To what extent do individuals' ambitions coincide with their potential?

— To what extent is each of my team members influenced in terms of his ambitions or aspirations, by family or friends?

— What formal discussions have I undertaken with each of my team members on his or her ambitions or aspirations and his or her own assessment of his or her training and development requirements?

No manager can *"guess"* his staffs' development needs or assess them on the basis of *"gut feel"*. Identification is achieved by personal communication.

A manager must be WILLING to take the time to review, on a constructive and regular basis, each of his staff's aspirations and ambitions. Such reviews can be challenging events because you are entering an area where emotion dominates.

I am sure that you have sat down with your team members on numerous occasions to assess their performance and the objectives you (and therefore the company) want them to achieve.

But when was the last occasion you sat down with an individual for the sole purpose of discussing his or her ambitions or aspirations?

To develop your company it is essential that you understand the motivations and aims of your staff. What may surprise you when you discuss this subject is that so many people have not determined their own ambitions or aspirations.

At this point let me draw a distinction between the words *"ambition"* and *"aspiration"*. For me ambition is the desire to take on greater responsibilities, authority and accountability in order to secure increased recognition and reward. Aspiration is the desire to continue working effectively at the present level, to assume no greater responsibility, authority or accountability and, as a consequence, forego additional or substantial reward.

My experience of working with people throughout the world has enabled me to see that whilst many people claim to be ambitious, in reality they are aspirants. Let's consider how you identify the ambitions and the aspirations of your team members.

I am going to introduce you to an approach I have used for many years with my own staff and it is based upon, what I often refer to as, my *"Five Magic Questions"*.

The approach I am going to outline is one I use with all members of staff after they have settled in to our company. I explain to each person that I am committed to developing all team members and want to ensure that whatever training is provided it is designed to help both the company and the individual achieve their respective objectives. Although I know what our company objectives are, I also need to be aware of each employee's goals. At this point I ask the employee this question:

> *During the course of your business career have you ever committed to paper your personal and career goals?*

Each person will have goals; 99 out of 100 people do not commit these goals to paper.

There can be various explanations for this situation. Perhaps some people have never thought about committing goals to paper? Perhaps some people consider the formality of writing down goals unnecessary? However, I suspect that for the majority of people who have thought about putting pen to paper that is as far as it has gone. Why? Because when you commit goals to paper you are holding yourself formally accountable. Accountability can, and often does, frighten people. If you retain your goals in your head then no one else is in a position to challenge directly what you have or have not achieved.

When I find that one of my team has not produced a formal career or personal development plan I advise him or her of the distinction I described earlier between ambition and aspiration. I want to gain my first indication of whether my team member is ambitious or not.

If the individual claims to be ambitious I invite him or her to undertake a project related to my five magic questions. I ask the person if he or she would be willing to commit to paper the answer to these questions:

> *What are my personal aspirations and ambitions for the next two/five/ ten years?*
>
> *How am I going to achieve these goals?*
>
> *By when am I going to achieve these goals?*
>
> *What will I gain if I achieve my goals?*
>
> *What will I lose if I achieve my goals?*

Do the questions appear to be simple ones? When I introduce people to them for the first time they often respond ... *"What's so magical about these questions? They look simple enough to me."* Yes, at first sight they may appear to be easy to answer. But they are not, as you will find as you learn more about each question.

Let's take question one:

> *What are my personal aspirations and ambitions for the next two, five or ten years?*

By the way, the timescale should be of your team member's own setting.

Now you have to consider such ancillary questions as:

> *Precisely what do I want to achieve?* Far too many people set vague or imprecise objectives. For example *"I want to get into Senior Management"* or *"I want to run my own business"*.
>
> *What are my personal goals and what are my professional goals?* Whilst the two are interlinked they are separate issues – and often conflicting in nature. For example, if your professional goal is to become Chief Executive of a large, multinational Engineering Company and your personal goal is to achieve a scratch handicap at golf, then the time demands of each are likely to be at variance.
>
> *Am I really ambitious?* Do I really want an increased workload, more

authority, more accountability, more pressure? What is really important to me? Professional and personal issues often conflict.

Let's look at question two:

How am I going to achieve these objectives?

It is one thing to know what you want to achieve – it is quite another to know how you will achieve these goals. When you are establishing career goals it is always desirable to seek the advice of those people whose professional experiences and opinions you respect on how goals can and should be pursued. The *"How"* question encourages an individual to consider not only the various actions he or she will need to take to achieve objectives but also whether he or she considers him or herself to be capable of achieving the goals.

Question three:

By when am I going to achieve these goals?

Regardless of the timescale you set goals will be achieved on a progressive basis. You need to set yourself demanding but realistic deadlines and you should treat the deadlines you set as sacrosanct. Too many people let deadlines slip and then rationalise their slippage with such remarks as:

Well I was only six months late

Given the ups and downs of life I guess a year here or there doesn't matter too much

Time is finite. You'll never get anymore of it and you can never recover lost time. So do everything within your power to hit your deadlines.

Questions four and five asked:

What will I gain if I achieve my goals?

and

What will I lose if I achieve my goals?

For the naïve employee promotion can only bring gains. His thoughts often turn to the material rewards associated with promotion – that increase in salary, bigger bonuses, larger car and so on.

But the gains for the ambitious include:

— increased responsibilities: you gain extra or more difficult work.

— increased authority: you gain extra decision-making rights.

— increased accountability: you have to account more often and in greater detail for your actions.

Question five is the one which surprises people most. It is all too easy to be blinded by the potential gains from achieving ambitions. But in business, as in life in general, for every gain there is an associated potential loss.

If you secure a Chief Executive's role in a multinational company, you may gain a high salary, beautiful car, impressive office and spacious home. But you may lose time with your family and friends, lose sleep, lose health and lose peace of mind.

As you encourage your staff to consider their future my five magic questions act like a mirror put up to the individual's face. As the individual considers the questions he takes a long look at himself in that imaginary mirror. As he continues to look the questions come thick and fast.

Your job is to offer to help all of your staff to understand the nature and extent of their ambitions and aspirations.

When they understand these, and share them with you, then you will know what you can and should do in terms of their training and development.

PART FOUR

EMPLOYEE DEVELOPMENT METHODS AND TECHNIQUES

Chapter 8

DO YOU REALISE THAT QUESTIONING IS YOUR MOST POWERFUL PERSONNEL DEVELOPMENT TOOL?

Perhaps you are surprised at the question itself. After all, isn't training the process of delivering information, conveying knowledge and developing skills. Yes, it is all of those things. However, questions are essential if you are to achieve success as a developer of people.

Questions are used to:

— help individuals recognise their strengths and shortcomings

— identify individuals' attitudes towards the information you are conveying

— test peoples' understanding and retention of training

— help people analyse their performance

— help people to propose their own solutions to the challenges they face

Too many managers are statement-orientated rather than question-orientated when they train. Such managers are members of the TELL THEM – DON'T ASK THEM school of training. They hold the view that if you talk at people positive change will result. Rarely is this the case. In 30 years of developing people I have found that statements create confrontation, whereas questions stimulate communication.

Consider your reaction if the person seeking to train and develop you were to say such things as:

I wouldn't do that if I were you

You will not succeed like that

I'm not impressed by the planning you've undertaken for . . .

You didn't handle that well

You need to better yourself

You need to learn new skills

You can convert these statements into questions and pose them in a passive and relaxed manner, for example:

What has lead you to consider that type of approach?

What level of success do you consider you will achieve from that approach?

How much time were you able to allocate to the preparation of...?

What importance do you attach to achieving greater success in your job?

How interested would you be in discovering new techniques that would help you to achieve even better results than you have in the past?

How did you think that went?

As a result of converting the statements into questions you can anticipate a far more positive dialogue.

While you should substitute questions for statements when you are training, you must seek to avoid the one prefix to a question that will undermine the effectiveness of your questioning.

This is the prefix: *WHY*. It has often been described as the most provocative word in the English language. Because however you express the word *WHY* it conveys criticism.

For example:

Why didn't you do that?

Why haven't you . . .?

Why can't you . . .?

Remember you can always substitute the word *WHAT* for *WHY*. Questions prefixed by *WHAT* are far less threatening and they can encourage the recipient of the question to give an open and more candid reply.

Let's consider the power of questioning in more detail. When developing your people you use two distinct types of question: these are STRUCTURED and UNSTRUCTURED questions. STRUCTURED QUESTIONS enable you to gather the maximum information in the minimum time.

Structured questions are those prefixed by the words:

"WHAT"	"WHO"	"HOW"
"WHERE"	"WHEN"	"TO WHAT EXTENT/DEGREE"

Any questions prefixed by these words cannot be answered by *"yes"* or *"no"*.

Unstructured questions are those prefixed by the words:

"DO YOU ..."	"ARE YOU ..."	"COULD YOU ..."
"HAVE YOU ..."	"WOULD YOU ..."	"WILL YOU ..."

These prefix lead to *"yes"* or *"no"* replies.

When training and developing your people there will be occasions when you will need to obtain a definitive *"yes"* or *"no"*. However, these are likely to be very much in the minority.

Developing people involves using questions to achieve a variety of objectives. You use them to check individuals' UNDERSTANDING of points you have conveyed, ACCEPTANCE of the ideas/suggestions you have put forward and willingness to APPLY the training you have given. You also use questions to prompt individuals to THINK about things for themselves. STRUCTURED QUESTIONS enable you to achieve these goals.

Before reviewing various situations in which you would use structured questions it is important to emphasise a key fact:

> UNDERSTANDING THE PRINCIPLE OF STRUCTURED QUESTIONING IS ONE THING – DEVELOPING THE SKILL IS QUITE ANOTHER.

Listed below are some of the ways in which you can develop your questioning skill.

1. Incorporate NUMERICAL QUALIFICATIONS within your questions.

   Shown below are some examples of numerical qualification questions:

   > *Jim, what do you consider to be the three biggest demands on your time?*
   >
   > *What do you consider to be the two most important issues facing our department?*
   >
   > *Shirley, what would be the three actions you would take to improve our customer service function?*

The introduction of a number increases the QUANTITY of information secured. However, it is important not to include too many numerical qualifications within a dialogue because the repetition can irritate your team member.

2. Develop the skill of SECONDARY QUESTIONING.

   When you ask your staff questions their responses can often be general or vague in nature. In these situations ask a secondary question to qualify or quantify your team member's initial reply. For example:

   Your first question: *"Bill, how will you apply the technique I've just demonstrated?"*

   Response: *"I will use it with my major prospective customers."*

   Your second question: *"In what specific ways?"*

   It is easy to become frustrated by less than complete responses. But do not show your frustration, let your secondary questions secure the response you require.

3. Ask PROBE questions.

   Probe questions are concerned with the identification of ATTITUDES, OPINIONS and VIEWS. When you want to identify individuals' real feelings towards the issues you are discussing ask such questions as:

   What is your attitude towards … ?

   What are your views on … ?

   What is your opinion of … ?

   Since so much of your training and development of people is concerned with stimulating positive attitudes and behaviours use probe questions regularly.

4. Use REVERSE QUESTIONING when you want to stimulate the thoughts of your people.

   When one of your team members approaches you with a particular difficulty and asks you *"What do you think I should do about … ?"* use the reverse question of … *"If I were not here, how would you tackle the issue?"* or *"What do you think is the best approach?"*

   You are not seeking to convey an unwillingness to give help. Instead you are encouraging your team member to analyse the issue for himself, consider alternative actions and make decisions. Developing people involves developing their capacity to determine their own actions.

As you seek to develop your questioning skills there are a number of easy traps into which you can fall. The first is that of asking INTERROGATIVE or STACCATO QUESTIONS. When you question your staff your aim must be to avoid sounding like a question master on a quiz show or a hostile interviewer. Link your questions with CONVERSATIONAL PRELUDES.

A conversational prelude is a series of words which precede your question and which relax your team member and justify your question. Here are some examples:

> *James, you are aware of the strengths of our main competitors, in view of this, what actions do you consider we should take to consolidate our position as market leader?*

> *Anne, there are various methods we could use to improve productivity, which do you think would be the most effective?*

The second trap is the inclusion of GENERAL or NEGATIVE WORDING within your questions. The general and negative words I am referring to include *"feel"*, *"hopefully"* and *"perhaps"*. Here are two examples of ineffective structured questions:

> *How do you feel things are going at the present time?*

That question is likely to elicit no more than *"OK"* or *"All right"* or *"Not bad"*.

The second example is:

> *Could I ask you what, hopefully, you expect to achieve from that approach?*

The question suggests you do not believe your team member's approach will work and that can encourage him to become defensive.

The previous example of an ineffective question leads me to the third trap, that of preceding a structured question with an unstructured prefix. When you ask ... *"Could I ask you what ... ?"* your listener often focuses on the phrase *"Could I ask you"* and he may reply *"No"*. You may consider the unstructured prefix to be a polite way to ask a question. It may be, but it is not an effective way. Substitute a conversational prelude for the unstructured prefix.

You will use STRUCTURED QUESTIONS for a variety of purposes as you seek to develop your staff. However, your most common requirement will be to achieve the following:

— to check individuals' UNDERSTANDING of the issues you have put forward

— to establish if they have ACCEPTED the ideas, suggestions and training you have put forward

— to ensure they will ACTION their acceptance

Teachers are full time trainers of our children and it is surprising how often teachers fail to check understanding, acceptance and action in their pupils. When they do seek to check they often resort to such questions as:

Was that clear David?

Did you understand that Brian?

Have you any questions about … ?

You can imagine the replies. No child likes to admit a lack of understanding – and nor do adults. Therefore, you need to ask your questions in a subtle way. Here are some examples:

What do you consider to be the main benefits of the approach I have outlined?

What do you believe we can achieve from adopting the ideas I have described?

Under what circumstances would you use the technique I have just demonstrated?

With which of your customers would you try the approach I have outlined?

When will you implement the new system?

Questions need to be asked in a relaxed manner and often preceded by a conversational prelude. Your questions will ensure you do not assume that your training has been understood, accepted and will be actioned. As we all know, if you assume it makes an ASS of U and ME!

For examples of questions used regularly by managers who successfully develop their team members refer to Checklist three on page 161.

CHAPTER 9

HOW TO PERSUADE YOUR STAFF TO WANT TO DO WHAT YOU WANT THEM TO DO

There is an old saying ... *"If you learn you earn"*.

Regrettably many people are defensive about learning new skills and one of your most important tasks, as a manager, is to help people to recognise that they have a NEED (an essential requirement) or a WANT (a desire) to learn and to develop.

How do you help people to recognise their need to change and to develop?

The answer lies in your most powerful training tool – your STRUCTURED QUESTIONS.

Before seeking to introduce your team members to new ideas, concepts and techniques ask yourself the following question:

> *What would encourage my team member to accept my ideas?*

You are seeking to identify in your mind your employee's potential needs and wants. Let me illustrate the process. You want to introduce one of your sales staff to a series of new approaches to handling customer objections and you ask yourself the question:

> *What would encourage him to accept my ideas?*

You consider his needs and wants could be:

— more sales

— more commission

— less rejections from customers

— more personal recognition within the company

Now you convert these assumptions into questions to pose to the sales person, for example:

> *What importance do you attach to increasing your sales this year?*

How much commission would you like to earn this year?

How do rejections from customers to your proposals affect you?

What value would you attach to heading next month's sales ladder?

Before presenting the new techniques you ask some, and possibly all, of the questions you have prepared. Your aim is to secure responses which enable you to summarise his requirements and stimulate his interest in listening to your ideas.

Shown below is an example of the summary technique:

Bill, from what you have said it would appear that you are very keen to increase your sales, and thereby your commission, this year and achieve a top three position on the sales ladder.

If I were to show you ways to achieve these goals I am sure you would be very interested.

The question is rhetorical. The sales person has provided you with the reasons for showing an interest in the training you wish to give. You can now proceed with the presentation of your ideas.

CHAPTER 10

HOW SHOULD YOU PRESENT YOUR IDEAS, CONCEPTS AND TECHNIQUES TO YOUR STAFF?

Do you have a favourite radio station? Most people do and the funny thing is that the majority of people share the same favourite. I am referring to radio station "W.I.I.F.M" – the most listened to station in the world and the one that never goes off the air.

W.I.I.F.M stands for ... *"What's In It For Me?"*

Whenever any of us are presented with a new product, a service or an idea we ask ourselves the question ... *"What's in it for me?"*

If the proposition matches our needs or wants then we are likely to accept it. However, many managers fail to recognise the importance of W.I.I.F.M when they are seeking to train and develop their staff.

Let me explain how you can put across your ideas, suggestions and recommendations in ways that demonstrate you are tuned in to your team member's favourite radio station.

Regardless of the nature of the training you give your staff it must contain three distinct components. These are:

What it is

What it does

What it will do for *you* specifically

The *"What it is"* component refers to the subject of your training. For example:

David, I want to introduce you to a range of time utilisation techniques.

The *"What it does"* element highlights the benefits your team member will derive from adopting the techniques. For example:

The techniques will enable you to achieve improved results within your department.

The *"What it does for you specifically"* comment is the personalising of your presentation. For example:

> *In addition, the techniques will help to relieve the pressure you have been experiencing during the last month.*

It is tempting for some managers to say to themselves:

> *All I need to do is explain what it is I want people to do – they can work out the benefits of adopting my suggestions for themselves.*

Whilst there is some truth in this assertion you may be surprised to find that on many occasions employees do not recognise or seek to identify the advantages they can gain from adopting new ideas. Therefore, do not be afraid to point out what you might consider to be obvious. What is obvious to one person may not be to another.

The extent to which you explain the benefits which can be derived from your training, ideas and suggestions depends upon your assessment of the attitudes of the person you are training. With this knowledge you can also decide whether you want to highlight advantages in terms of what the person can GAIN from adopting the ideas or what he could LOSE from not following your suggestions.

Each of your team members is motivated to accept (or reject) your ideas by different factors. Many people want to know what they will gain from your training, advice and recommendations. On the other hand a significant number of people are far more concerned with what they will lose if they do not adopt your recommendations.

If you ensure you are tuned into your team member's radio station and consistently explain what is in it for them, then you will persuade individuals to want to do what you want them to do. Employees will develop and so too will your business results and ultimately your profitability.

CHAPTER 11

HOW GOOD A LISTENER ARE YOU?

Developing people is not just about imparting information – that is the act of talking at people. You develop people by talking with them and that necessitates listening.

At this point let me draw a distinction between hearing and listening. We are all born with the capacity to hear. It is an intuitive act. We don't need to tune our ears in every time we want to hear something. We don't need to think to hear. Listening, on the other hand, does require us to think. We have to concentrate on a variety of issues including:

- what is being said
- how information is conveyed
- what is not being said
- why something is being said
- whether what is said is what is meant

If you wish to get the best out of the people who work with and for you then you will need to become an ACTIVE LISTENER.

When you are listening actively you:

- demonstrate attentive posture. This involves you moving or leaning towards your team member if you are sitting behind a desk.
- don't doodle or fidget
- look at your contact all the time. I do not mean stare, but as you would when you are in conversation with a close friend.
- give the occasional nod
- smile in agreement
- convey an interested tone of voice
- ask questions
- express compliments
- look for your team member's non-verbal communication signals. Your

team member's attitude is often expressed through his or her body language.

Listening is a conscious activity and one which can be influenced by distractions or self-created barriers. I am referring to such things as prejudice, disinterest, fatigue, assumptive thinking and personality variances.

Listening shows you are interested in your team members and if you show your interest in them they are more likely to show an interest in the issues you want to discuss and goals you want them to achieve.

CHAPTER 12

ARE YOU A WHAT OR A HOW MANAGER?

Managers can be classified as either WHAT or HOW managers and regrettably, in my experience, the majority appear to be WHAT managers.

The WHAT manager is the individual who believes that improving company performance is achieved by the simple task of telling people WHAT to do.

Shown below is a dialogue between a WHAT manager and one of his team:

Manager	*Right Brian, what I want you to do is improve productivity by 10% this quarter, so get to it*
Team Member	*10%, but how?*
Manager	*That's up to you*
Team Member	*But 10%, that's a tough target*
Manager	*Yes, but that's what you have to achieve*
Team Member	*I'd still like your thoughts on how the increase can be achieved*
Manager	*Look, I'm here to tell you want needs to be done, not to show you how*

It would not, of course, be productive to spoon feed your staff with ideas. However, whenever you ask someone to do something new, different, more challenging and demanding you cannot abdicate your responsibility to show your team members HOW to fulfil the responsibility.

So why do so many managers adopt the *"this is what I want you to do"* style, rather than the *"let me show you how to"* style?

The main reason is managers' inner fear of having to DEMONSTRATE a new or different skill.

There is a fundamental difference between knowing WHAT needs to be done and showing someone HOW to do it.

I have worked with thousands of sales people over the last 30 years and on more occasions than I care to recall many of these people have said such things as the following to me:

> *You know my boss is always telling me I need to be better at handling customer objections. I know he's right, but he never shows me how.*

or

> *My Sales Manager spends time accompanying me on both existing and prospective customer calls and it's always the same story – what you need to be is more assertive, quicker on your feet, a better listener. You name the weakness I seem to have it. But does he ever show me how to improve my performance? Never. Even when I put him on the spot.*

Developing people to develop your company obligates you to DEMONSTRATE the skills you want your staff to master.

CHAPTER 13

ARE YOU WILLING TO ACCEPT YOUR TEAM MEMBERS' *"MONKEYS"*?

MANAGING rather than DOING is one of the factors in the growth and success of companies. By this phrase I mean that managers apply themselves to achieving results THROUGH their people. These managers do not consider that their position requires them to take on the heaviest of workloads by undertaking their staff's jobs.

Managers who manage develop their people to solve their own problems and they often do this by introducing them to the concept of *"Passing the Monkey"*.

Passing the Monkey was developed in the United States by The William Oncken Company some years ago and it remains totally relevant to business today.

Let me introduce you to the concept of *"Passing the Monkey"*.

Can you recognise and relate to this scene?

You are leaving your office and one of your team members runs up to you. *"Glad I've caught you,"* he says, *"we've got a problem."* You know enough about the matter in question to get involved, but insufficient to make an instant decision. So the conversation ends with you saying *"OK, leave it with me. I'll get back to you"*.

Who is delegating to whom?

Who is invading whose time?

So who or what is *"the monkey"*?

A MONKEY is defined as *"whatever the next move is at the end of a dialogue"*. In the example quoted, where was the monkey and where is it now?

If you manage (or perhaps I could say *"should manage"*) just six people, and each person passes you just one monkey, each day of the working week, then by Friday afternoon, you will have collected thirty monkeys!

Now monkeys need feeding. Do you think you'll have time to do your own work, when you have thirty hungry monkeys to feed?

If you continue to accept responsibility for the monkeys, and yet you have insufficient time to feed them, then they will die. Thirty problems, no solutions and a manager who becomes known as the individual around which everything withers and dies!

How do you deal with the monkeys, develop your people and achieve effective use of your time?

Follow these guidelines when educating your team to appreciate the value of time and the importance of accepting responsibility:

— Explain to each of your team members the concept of *"passing the monkey"* – explain that whilst you will help each person to find his or her solutions to problems, at no time will you allow the monkey to find a resting place on YOUR shoulders.

— Explain that the word *"WE"* is not a transfer device that you will either recognise or accept.

— Advise each person that you have no objection to them bringing *"monkeys"* to you – PROVIDED they are accompanied by proposed solutions and timetables.

When many managers are learning HOW to delegate, they become concerned about the risk of losing control. Their staff may make mistakes. The answer is to take out a form of *"insurance policy"*.

Here are your INSURANCE POLICIES FOR MONKEYS:

— Where the risk is LOW, take out an inexpensive policy – that is one with a low premium, in terms of time. Tell your team member ... *"Act on your own, but let me know what you are doing."*

— Where the risk is HIGHER, you should take out a medium priced policy, one which is more expensive in terms of time. Tell your team member ... *"Act on your own initiative, but report to me regularly."*

— Where the risk is GREAT, take out an expensive policy which can eliminate all risk. Tell your team member ... *"Decide upon a course of action and return with your recommendations."*

If you use your time to train your team members in the care and feeding of monkeys then they will become more confident and decisive. And you will find that you are working with them and not for them.

CHAPTER 14

HOW CAN YOU TRAIN YOUR TEAM MEMBERS TO SOLVE THEIR OWN PROBLEMS?

In the previous chapter you were introduced to a process which will reduce the number of occasions on which your staff bring you problems they wish to place on your shoulders. This chapter describes how you can develop individuals, and your team as a whole, to solve their own problems.

Within most companies an enormous amount of time is devoted to *"solving problems"*. Regrettably the ways in which the solutions are sought are often less than systematic and the results of the deliberations disappointing.

However, by applying my PSF approach you can ensure problems are addressed systematically. PSF stands for PROBLEM SOLVING FORMULA.

The formula requires the problem solver to undertake seven activities, which are set out below:

1. DEFINE THE PROBLEM

This is a far more difficult task than you might consider.

Unless you identify the true nature of the problem you may spend a considerable amount of time addressing the wrong solution.

2. IDENTIFY THE EFFECTS OF THE PROBLEM

It is not the problem itself which concerns people – it is how the individual or group is affected by the problem.

When you have defined the problem produce a list of the effects. They may be relatively minor in nature and not warrant a great deal of time being spent on finding a detailed solution to the problem.

3. LIST THE CAUSES OF THE PROBLEM

Business problems rarely have one cause. Therefore, it is important to identify all of the contributory factors. However, care should be taken to ensure the discussion on the causes does not turn into a hunt for a person (or persons) to blame.

4. BRAINSTORM ALTERNATIVE SOLUTIONS

Too many people look for *"quick fix solutions"* to their business problems and they often approach the identification of a solution by asking themselves the following:

> *Have I experienced this problem (or something similar) before?*

If they respond to their own question with a *"yes"* they advance to:

> *How did I solve it last time?*

and

> *Did my solution work?*

If the answer to the last question is once again *"yes"*, or even a qualified *"Well, just about"*, then the previous solution is often repeated.

Although I am not dismissing the value of reflection there are enormous benefits to be gained from opening one's mind to new solutions. By releasing those mental shackles new approaches can be identified.

5. WEIGH UP THE ALTERNATIVES

Your brainstorming should produce a range of alternative solutions. These need to be assessed in terms of practicality and viability. Pragmatism has to be applied to your final choice of actions to resolve your problem.

6. ACTION YOUR SOLUTION

In my experience far too many managers arrive at a solution to their problem and then fail to action that solution. Is it nervousness? Is it a fear of failure? Is it an inclination to procrastinate?

Management is about making decisions and acting upon these decisions. Therefore, ACT. Hesitation could compromise your chances of success.

7. MONITOR AND EVALUATE PROGRESS

It is essential that you monitor the progress of your problem-solving actions and evaluate whether your solutions prove to be effective.

PSF can be used by individuals, but I have found that its value is most clearly recognised when used by a group.

When you train your team to use the Problem Solving Formula it is important to remind them of the following ground rules:

- An agreed amount of time should be allocated to the PSF exercise and this should not be exceeded unless there are exceptional circumstances.

Without a defined time allocation discussion can be protracted and not focused.

- Once the group has decided upon how much time it will allocate to the PSF exercise then specific time periods should be allocated to stages one to six of the PSF. For example, if two hours have been allocated to the project then the six stages might be allocated by the group as follows:

Defining the problem	10 minutes
Identifying the effects of the problem	15 minutes
Identifying the causes of the problem	15 minutes
Brainstorming alternative solutions	30 minutes
Weighing up the alternatives	30 minutes
Producing an Action Plan	20 minutes

- The person selected to chair the group must exercise strict control over timekeeping. The time allocations for each stage of the PSF exercise should be treated as sacrosanct.

The use of PSF will not guarantee that you or your team members will solve every business problem encountered. However, this systematic approach will increase your chances of success and, in the end, will save you time.

Developing your people to solve their own problems is an important part of your managerial role and one from which you should obtain considerable satisfaction.

Chapter 15

DEVELOPING YOUR TEAM MEMBERS TO MAXIMISE THE RETURN THEY OBTAIN ON THEIR USE OF THEIR BUSINESS TIME

Time is one of our most precious possessions. It is irreplaceable and has often been described as *"the most valuable thing a man can spend"* as this riddle highlights:

> *What is the longest and yet shortest thing in the world?*
>
> *What is the fastest and yet slowest?*
>
> *What is the most divisible and the most extended?*
>
> *What is the least valued?*
>
> *What is the most regretted?*
>
> *What devours everything?*
>
> *The answer is TIME*

Regrettably many managers and employees underestimate the value of their time. If you are to develop your company then you need to develop your team members' appreciation of the value of time and their ability to use it to the maximum advantage.

In this chapter you will be introduced to a number of ways in which you can develop the time utilisation skills of your team. Incidentally, many of the managers with whom I have worked have asked me if I could make them *"better at time management"*. My response to these requests has always been the same – *"I cannot make you better at managing time. Because you cannot manage time, you can only manage yourself more effectively."*

The process of helping your team members to make better use of their time should start with you making each person aware of a number of (tongue in cheek) factors relating to time that they may not recognise or appreciate.

For example:

- — Time never stands still. Although so many of us often make statements to the contrary.
- — Time never flies. It moves at a constant speed.
- — We all have time. Although we often complain that we have none.
- — Now is all the time we have at our command. The time that has passed is history and the time still to come is only assumption.
- — Time will control you if you do not control it. It is not the hours we put into our day that are important – it is what we put into those hours.

So how can your team utilise their time more effectively? Shown below and overleaf are six actions they can take:

1. Since each person cannot increase the amount of time that is available to him or her it is essential he or she INCREASES THE VALUE OF EACH HOUR WORKED. This means that each person should be planning his or her work with the following question in mind:

   What value will the activity I am proposing to undertake bring to my company?

   It is very easy to fill your time with jobs – but these may be of little or no value to your company.

2. Each person should seek to be PRO-ACTIVE rather than reactive in his or her use of time. Being pro-active involves an individual seeking to plan and organise his or her work. Reactive time utilisation involves waiting for things to happen and then responding. If you are pro-active you are directing your efforts to actions that can positively benefit your company. Reactive employees tend to be people who see their jobs as that of a *"problem-solver"*.

3. Each person should seek to avoid CRISES destroying his or her time planning.

   Crises can and do occur in today's hectic business world. However, well-trained employees examine the causes of their crises and determine actions they can take to avoid similar crises occurring again.

4. Each person should seek to avoid the TELEPHONE destroying his or her time planning.

   The telephone has been described as:

   > *The greatest nuisance among conveniences and the greatest convenience among nuisances*

Train your staff to apply my TEA formula when they use the telephone:

Tell people what you want

Explain why you want it

Action the agreements you reach

5. When your staff are called upon to deal with a great deal of paperwork in their jobs encourage them to use my AID formula. AID is an acronym for ACTION, INFORMATION and DEFER. Action items are ones that need immediate attention. Information items can be put to one side for reading between important activities. Deferred items can be put in a desk drawer for moments when the individual wants some light reading.

6. Each person should follow the *"DO IT TO THE FINISH"* and *"HANDLE IT JUST ONCE"* approach to his or her work.

   I appreciate that it is not always possible to complete a task in one attempt. However, the principle is based upon individuals focusing their efforts on the issue of the moment, thereby avoiding distractions.

   The *"HANDLE IT JUST ONCE"* approach also encourages individuals to be disciplined in the way they tackle their tasks.

Explain to your staff that successful companies contain individuals who understand and apply themselves to the definitions of EFFICIENCY and EFFECTIVENESS.

EFFICIENCY is doing the job right.

EFFECTIVENESS is doing the right job.

The late Professor Northcote Parkinson created his own *"Law"* relating to time utilisation. It is … *"work expands so as to fill the time available for its completion."*

Through guiding, coaching and counselling your staff you can ensure the corollary to Parkinson's Law is applied in your company:

> *Work can be made to contract to free the time which would otherwise not be made available.*

CHAPTER 16

DO YOU REALLY UNDERSTAND HOW TO GET THE BEST OUT OF THE PEOPLE WHO WORK WITH AND FOR YOU?

Let's take a fresh look at another aspect of your responsibility to develop your staff – your responsibility to MOTIVATE and avoid DEMOTIVATING each member of your team.

Many books have been written on the subject of MOTIVATION and I would encourage you to read as many as you can on the subject. However, this chapter will focus your attention not on the subject of how to motivate people, but on a much more important issue – how to avoid DEMOTIVATING people.

If managers concentrate more of their efforts on removing the causes of demotivation amongst their staff then results will improve significantly.

I am not suggesting that you should avoid implementing motivational ideas. What I am expressing is the warning that whatever form of motivation you may use will be only TEMPORARY in nature. Causes of demotivation tend to last much longer.

Companies around the world spend millions of pounds on motivational schemes and it disappoints me to find that so much of this expenditure produces little long term return for the company. Some years ago a client company of mine took its top five sales staff and their partners to the West Indies for a ten day, all expenses paid, holiday. The company held the view that it was important to recognise individuals' outstanding achievements. I certainly supported that assertion. The company believed that the West Indies holiday would be a *"great motivator"* which would enthuse the sales staff to achieve even better results in the year ahead. However, people are fickle and it was revealed that just a day after the five sales staff returned to work one was heard saying to another:

> *It was really penny-pinching of the company to only put us in a four star rather than five star hotel, and why didn't we each get a suite rather than just an ocean view room?*

In response his colleague said:

> *Yes, good points, and my wife thought we should have been taken to the airport in a limousine.*

The fact that neither man could have afforded the trip if they had been required to pay seemed to slip their mind. They were looking for faults and as their conversation extended the motivational effect of the holiday had been replaced with demotivation.

So what can you do to address the issue of DEMOTIVATION? The starting point is for you to take a long and hard look at your own company. What are the major causes of employee demotivation?

Observation and passive listening will not provide you with the answers you need. You must seek out the views of your team members in a positive manner.

I have found that, in the majority of departments, individual discussions are a more successful means of receiving feedback than group discussions. The latter can, even when conducted by the most skilled of managers, become moan and groan sessions with little objective discussion.

When conducting discussions with your team members follow these guidelines:

1. Set the scene for each discussion by explaining that your primary objective is to identify those factors within your department or the company (and that includes yourself) that are having a negative influence on your team member's attitude, in order that these can be addressed quickly.

2. Seek to avoid over-using the word *"demotivation"*. Substitute such words as *"issues"*, *"difficulties"*, *"disappointments"*. You need to identify negative matters. However, you want to approach them in a positive way and the word demotivation has only negative connotations.

3. Do not make rash promises about the actions you, or others, will or may take as a result of your discussion. Your safest course of action is always to say that you will consider each issue raised and reach, or seek, the appropriate decision by a targeted date.

4. Do not put words in your team members' mouths by using LEADING QUESTIONS. Here are three examples of leading questions:

    What has the most negative influence on your attitudes as you fulfil your job, is it the cramped working conditions?

    Which aspects of your job do you find least satisfying, is it the amount of time you have to spend in front of your computer screen?

    If you had the opportunity to make one big change to how we run the department what would it be, a reduction in the number of meetings we have?

Allow people free expression of their views through the use of STRUCTURED QUESTIONS.

5. Be seen to be taking NOTES during each discussion. Your staff will expect you to be showing a real interest in their replies.

As you examine the causes of demotivation within your business you may be surprised to find that monetary issues do not represent as big a cause of demotivation as you might have imagined. Checklist numbers four and five on pages 162 and 167 reveal a range of powerful demotivators. Each of these sources can and should be addressed urgently. But do not be fooled into thinking that once they have been addressed they can be forgotten. Managerial life just isn't that simple.

Once a source of demotivation is removed (or at least its effects reduced) then another can, and often does, take its place. As a consequence it is little wonder that so many managers can be heard to say … *"Aren't my staff ever happy?"*

You must aim to be sensitive to atmospheres within your team and you should encourage people to talk with you about the issues which are affecting their motivation. You are not seeking to create a moan and misery mentality amongst your team but an open and constructive dialogue.

The fact that you are prepared to acknowledge that no company or individual is perfect and, therefore, demotivation can be created, will be appreciated by your team members. In addition your actions to eliminate sources of demotivation will demonstrate to individuals that your interest is real and that you are not just going through the motions of showing interest in your team.

Refer to Checklist fourteen on page 184 to examine your ability to provide your team members with consistent job satisfaction.

Chapter 17

A CHAIN IS ONLY AS STRONG AS ITS WEAKEST LINK

I am sure you will recall the saying shown above and my reason for reminding you of it is its relevance to developing your company.

What is a company? No more or less than a collection of people drawn together under the banner of a specific collective name.

How well that company performs depends on a multitude of factors. But arguably the most important factors are the confidence and competence of employees. That confidence and competence is revealed by how well people work together.

Is there genuine TEAMWORK within your company?

I define TEAMWORK as follows:

> *A group of people working together towards a common goal, in an atmosphere of mutual support and understanding.*

Why is TEAMWORK so important?

You may consider the question an obvious one, since so many managers are of the view that they already have a *"team"* of people who recognise the value of working together. Regrettably the reality is often somewhat different. Many companies are not comprised of teams – they employ collections of individuals. And those individuals do not recognise or accept the importance of teamwork.

Teamwork is important because it:

— creates a sense of belonging

— provides a common focus

— enables individuals to seek the support of others

— expands individuals' knowledge and skills

— enables individuals to utilise their different strengths

— enables a company to achieve and sustain successful results

However, teamwork depends upon the group comprising individuals with mixed personalities and styles. Groups of people who share the same or very similar characteristics rarely achieve outstanding results.

Dr Meredith Belbin has been one of the leading researchers into the characteristics of employees and how they act or react in team situations. He has identified eight distinct categories of employee. They are:

COMPANY WORKER
CHAIRMAN
SHAPER
PLANT
RESOURCE INVESTIGATOR
MONITOR EVALUATOR
TEAM WORKER
COMPLETER FINISHER

What are the characteristics displayed by individuals in each of these categories? Here are Dr Belbin's descriptions:

1. THE COMPANY WORKER (CW)

The Company Worker turns concepts and plans into practical working procedures and carries out agreed plans systematically and efficiently.

The typical features of a Company Worker are:	Conservative, dutiful, predictable, stable, controlled.
Positive qualities:	Organising ability, practical common sense, hard working, self discipline, sincere, trustful.
Allowable weaknesses:	Lack of flexibility, unresponsiveness to unproven ideas, needs to work within stable structures.
Characteristic behaviours:	Transforming the concepts and ideas of others into practical courses of action. Commenting on what is and what is not feasible. Tailoring suggestions to make them fit into agreed plans and established systems.

The Company Worker should be given a job with a high measure of direct responsibility. He or she should take a major part in implementing the group's decisions.

2. THE CHAIRMAN (CH)

He or she controls the way in which a team moves towards the group objectives by making the best use of the team's resources. He or she recognises where the team's strengths and weaknesses lie and ensures that the best use is made of each team member's potential.

The typical features of a Chairman are:	Calm, self confident, controlled, authoritative but not autocratic.
Positive qualities:	Has a capacity for treating and welcoming all potential contributors on their merits and without prejudice. Has a strong sense of objectives.
Allowable weaknesses:	No more than ordinary in terms of intellect or creative ability.
Characteristic behaviour:	Clarifying group goals and objectives. Selecting problems on which decisions have to be made. Establishing priorities. Helping to establish group roles and responsibilities. Helping to define group boundaries. Summing up group feelings and achievements. Articulating group verdicts.

The team member with the highest Chairman score should take the part of the Team Leader even though he or she may not necessarily have the highest status in the group. If instead of a Chairman a Shaper is chosen to lead the team, then the Chairman should be designated to steer the group's activities.

3. THE SHAPER (SH)

He or she shapes the way in which the team effort is applied. He or she directs attention generally to the setting of objectives and priorities and seeks to impose some shape or pattern on group discussion and on the outcome of the group activities.

The typical features of a Shaper are:	Highly strung, outgoing, dynamic, dominant, impulsive.
Positive qualities:	Drive and readiness to challenge inertia, ineffectiveness, complacency or self deception. Does not harbour grudges.
Allowable weaknesses:	Prone to provocation, irritation and impatience.
Characteristic behaviour:	Shaping roles, boundaries, responsibilities, objectives and tasks. Looking for patterns in

group discussions. Propelling the group towards agreements of policy and action towards making decisions.

Shapers are used where goal-orientated activities are required or where a team needs to be galvanised into action. However, it may be necessary to balance the enthusiasm of a Shaper with the interpersonal skills of a Team Worker.

4. THE PLANT (PL)

The Plant is an individual who advances new ideas and strategies with special attention to major issues. He or she looks for possible breaks in the approach to the problems with which the group is confronted.

The typical features of a Plant are:	Individualistic, serious-minded, unorthordox, an ideas person, responds to praise.
Positive qualities:	High IQ, imagination, knowledge.
Allowable weaknesses:	Up in the clouds, inclined to disregard practical details or protocol, can make careless mistakes, can be sensitive to criticism.
Characteristic behaviour:	Puts forward suggestions. Comments constructively and then proposes counter suggestions. Offers new insights into lines of action already agreed.

The Plant should be allocated an innovative or strategic role. Some friction or other difficulties may occur if there are two Plants within a single group.

5. THE RESOURCE INVESTIGATOR (RI)

The Resource Investigator explores and reports on ideas, developments and resources outside of the group. He or she creates external contacts that may be useful to the team and conducts any subsequent negotiations.

Typical features of the Resource Investigator are:	Extrovert, enthusiastic, curious, communicative, stable, relaxed, sociable.
Positive qualities:	A capacity for contacting people and exploring anything new. An ability to respond to challenge.
Allowable Weaknesses:	Liable to lose interest once the initial fascinations have passed. Can be mistaken as the ideas person but lacks the originality that distinguishes the Plant.

Characteristic Behaviour:	Introducing external ideas and developments to the group. Contacting other individuals or groups on own initiative. Undertaking bargaining type activities.

The Resource Investigator should be encouraged to foster contacts and links outside the confines of the group and to import useful ideas and information. (The Monitor Evaluator can then assess their usefulness to the group.)

6. THE MONITOR EVALUATOR (ME)

The Monitor Evaluator analyses problems and evaluates ideas and suggestions so that the team is better placed to take balanced decisions.

Typical features of the Monitor Evaluator are:	Sober, unemotional, prudent, high IQ, dispassionate.
Positive qualities:	Judgement, discretion, hard-headedness, assimilation.
Allowable weaknesses:	Lacks inspiration or the ability to motivate others. Can be competitive with those who overlap him or her, for example, the Chairman or Plant.
Characteristic Behaviour:	Analysing problems and situations. Interpreting complex materials and clarifying obscurities. Assessing the judgements and contributions of others.

The Monitor Evaluator should approve all new plans. If a plan is not endorsed by the Monitor Evaluator then the group should proceed with caution.

7. THE TEAM WORKER (TW)

The Team Worker supports the team members in their strengths (e.g. builds on suggestions) and underpins them in their shortcomings. Improves communications between members. Fosters team spirit generally.

Typical features of the Team Worker are:	Socially orientated, rather mild, sensitive, loyal to the team.
Positive qualities:	An ability to respond to people and to situations, and to promote team spirit. Good listener.
Allowable weaknesses:	Indecisive at moments of crisis. Does not like confrontation.

Characteristic behaviour:	Providing personal support and assistance to others. Building on or endorsing other members ideas and suggestions. Encouraging contributions from the reticent. Taking steps to avert or overcome disruption of the team.

Team Workers should be allocated to supporting roles. It can be useful to have several Team Workers in one group.

8. THE COMPLETER FINISHER (CF)

The Completer Finisher focuses upon order and the completing of activities:

A typical feature of a Completer Finisher is:	Anxious introvert.
Positive qualities:	Self control and attention to detail.
Allowable weaknesses:	Worries about what might go wrong.
Characteristic behaviour:	Compulsive about order. Moves the group towards action and focuses the group on the accuracy of details.

Completer Finishers help to see things through to a finish. However, they can be impatient and intolerant of more casual members of the team.

How can you identify into which of the eight categories your staff fall?
The first way is to listen to how each person communicates.
The phrases below are indicative and representative of the kinds of behaviour associated with each of the Belbin Team roles.

COMPANY WORKER

Given the time we've got we could …

We can certainly do X within our budget

Let's get this on board

If we nail that part down we'll be more sure of this result

CHAIRMAN

What we are here to do is …

Let's do this first and that later

To summarise, the main points seem to be …

Perhaps you could … then he will …

To get back to the main issue would you …

SHAPER

What we have to do is …

We're wasting time – we have to …

No – you're wrong – the most important issue is …

If we put what you've said with his suggestion we can …

PLANT

What about …

Let's get underneath that …

It ought to be orange

Turning that on it's head gives us …

Why don't we go back to basics?

RESOURCE INVESTIGATOR

What a great idea …

I know someone who can …

Thunderflashes – no problem – my cousin …

I can persuade sales to …

MONITOR EVALUATOR

The problem with …

We have to watch out for …

Let's not overlook …

If we pay attention to the gist of this we should …

TEAM WORKER

Joe – I think you should listen to Harry

Let's give Frank's idea a chance

No need to fight about …

When Fred gets back from the hospital we could …

COMPLETER FINISHER

Let me check that ...

We'll never ... unless ...

What about ...

No ... we must check everything – to get it work

What about article 3 in sub-paragraph iv) paragraph G, in the ninth volume?

You can't do that – we'll be a week late

You can also obtain an indication of each of your staffs predominant characteristics by using Dr Belbin's questionnaire which is shown in Appendix three of this book, page 151.

Once you have produced a profile of your staff, what actions do you need to take to develop individuals to become a team?

Here are my top fourteen recommendations:

1. Seek to recruit individuals with mixed personalities and style. Do not recruit "in your image" or individuals who all demonstrate "Yes, Sir" tendencies.
2. Ensure each person understands his or her role and the standards they are expected to achieve. It is essential that each of your staff has a comprehensive Job Description which contains Key Tasks and the Minimum Standards of Performance you expect the individual to achieve when fulfilling each key task.
3. Encourage mutual respect within the group. Remind people that their different personalities and styles are strengths and not shortcomings.
4. Keep your group focused upon shared goals.
5. Stimulate individuals' desire to challenge and be challenged. Constructive debate on how things are or should be done is healthy within a group.
6. Encourage the group to be solution rather than problem orientated. Refer to Chapter Six, in Part Four of this book, for my Problem Solving Formula.
7. Establish clear and consistent lines of communication within the group.
8. Do not tolerate in-fighting amongst the group.
9. Encourage individuals to use a *"we"* and *"us"* style of communication rather than a *"me"*, *"my"* and *"I"* approach.
10. Seek group action commitments as well as individual action commitments.
11. Stimulate individuals' desire to learn from one another. Encourage

individuals to ask each other for advice and for feedback on their performance.

12. Remind your staff that they can each achieve successful results. However, when talents are combined successful results can be multiplied.
13. Encourage individuals to understand other team members' attitudes and perspectives. Differences can be unifying and not divisive features.
14. Set *"Standards of Excellence"* to which all members of the team will be committed.

Successful teams demonstrate skills in each of the following areas:

ORGANISING
EXPLORING
MONITORING
CONTROLLING
SUPPORTING

Exploring skills provide a team with ideas and contacts. The team roles which contribute to exploring skills are the PLANT (PL) and the RESOURCE INVESTIGATOR (RI).

If exploring skills are to be exploited properly by the team they have to be organised by a CHAIRMAN (CH) who is the diplomat of the group, and by a COMPANY WORKER (CW) who is the planner.

Organisation does not get things done, it only eases the way. To get things done you need controlling skills. The SHAPER (SH) get things done by leading from the front. Shapers are often impatient to produce visible results.

Without monitoring skills teams often get the wrong things done and often fail to complete tasks fully. This essential area is looked after by the MONITOR EVALUATOR (ME) and COMPLETER FINISHER (CF). The Monitor Evaluator makes sure that standards are maintained. But he or she can be over critical. The Completer Finisher is the dotter of the I's and the crosser of the T's.

Support skills are important and the relevant team role is the TEAM WORKER (TW). The Team Worker enjoys warm and friendly work groups and tries to establish stable working relationships.

Team working and team spirit do not just happen – they are created as a result of a great deal of hard work. However, you know you are on the road to success when your people demonstrate the 3C's. I am referring to:

CONFIDENCE
COMPETENCE
CONSISTENCY

Refer to Appendix four: *"Useful people to have in teams"*.

CHAPTER 18

HOW CAN YOU INCENTIVIZE YOUR TEAM MEMBERS AND STIMULATE THEIR PERFORMANCE?

Look around your present team. Do they all think and act in the same way? Of course not. For these reasons no two people can be stimulated equally by precisely the same form of incentive.

One of your important and ongoing tasks is to consider very carefully the type and extent of any incentive process you adopt for your team members.

Some years ago an Italian psychologist called Tosti developed a checklist (which he titled *"Tosti's Taxonomy"*) of the categories of employee incentive.

The way to use his checklist (which is shown below) is to:

— put an individual from within your team in your mind.

— mark the incentives you consider would be most appreciated by that person, and which you can offer given your resources (including your time and energy).

— check out your understanding by offering an incentive for some job well done or by discussing your selection with the employee and making an informal contract.

REMEMBER, EACH MEMBER OF YOUR TEAM HAS A UNIQUE VALUE SYSTEM. Different people see different things as rewards. Furthermore, people change their value systems. What may be seen as reward by one person today may be less exciting to the same person another day.

Here is Tosti's Taxonomy:

1. RECOGNITION

— Personal praise

— Tangible awards

— Certification of accomplishment

— Formal public acknowledgement (for example, testimonials and plaques)

- Informal acknowledgements (i.e., *"a pat on the back"*)
- Letters of appreciation
- Publicity (for example, personal notes in the company newsletter or the *"employee of the month"* postings)
- Selection to represent the team at company meetings or conferences

2. JOB RESPONSIBILITIES

- The opportunity for more self management
- More power to decide and/or implement (i.e. the scope of the job)
- More frequent decision-making or participation in decision-making
- More frequent requests to provide input for decisions
- Greater opportunity to schedule time (for example to set his or her own priorities)
- Greater access to information

3. STATUS INDICATORS

- A larger work area
- A promotion
- A more private office
- Receiving more or newer equipment
- Status symbols (for example, type and size of office, windows, carpeting, nameplate, plants, desks)
- Invitations to *"high-level"* meetings
- A new job title
- Being placed in a special grading
- A different type of company car

4. TANGIBLE REWARDS

- Cash bonuses
- Commissions
- Profit sharing
- Piece work pay
- Merit increases

— Lunch on the company

— Paid trips to professional meetings

— Company donations to a charity in the employee's name

— Increased *"fringe benefits"* (for example, life insurance, private petrol)

5. SOCIAL ACTIVITIES

— Talking to fellow employees (for example, work or coffee groups)

— Special lunches

— Going to company outings or parties

— Going to company organised recreational activities (for example, football team)

— Having the boss listen to problems with interest

— Dinner (lunch, drinks or just coffee) with the boss (and partner)

6. INCENTIVE FEEDBACK

— Increased knowledge of the company's financial situation

— Graphs of progress

— Receiving knowledge on the quality and quantity of his/her work

— Receiving *"fan mail"* (for example, customer compliments)

7. JOB TASKS

— Assignment of new duties

— Re-design of present job

— Frequent changes of duties

— Assignment of preferred work partners

— Approval of job related requests

— Rapid follow up by boss on job related problems

— Opportunities for advanced training

8. RELIEF FROM THE LEAST POPULAR POLICIES OR PROCEDURES

— Exemption from time clocks

— Exemption from selected company control policies

— Exemption from close supervision

— Relief from the threat of dismissal, loss of pay, or probationary status

9. RELIEF FROM AN UNPOPULAR WORK ENVIRONMENT

— Better lighting

— A move to a less noisy location

— A transfer from uncongenial workmates or a supervisor

— A move to a warmer or cooler work area

— A move closer to *"comfort"* facilities (for example, rest rooms, cafeteria, coffee machine)

10. PERSONAL ACTIVITIES

— Taking a longer break or receiving additional breaks or longer lunch times

— Leaving work earlier

— Time off, with, or without, pay

— Privileges (for example, phone calls, opportunity to travel, reserved parking)

By taking an active and consistent interest in your staff you will be able to identify and apply incentives that can have an important influence upon the performance of your team members.

CHAPTER 19

HOW OFTEN DO YOU USE TEAM MEETINGS AS A VEHICLE FOR DEVELOPING YOUR STAFF?

Hundreds of thousands of pounds are spent each week in the UK by managers holding meetings – and the sad fact is that much of this money is wasted. The reasons are numerous, as you will learn in this chapter. However, meetings can and should provide a wonderful vehicle for developing staff.

Think back to the last three meetings you conducted with your staff. How long did each meeting last? How much did it cost your company in direct and indirect costs? What did you achieve as a result of the meeting? In what specific ways did your team benefit from their attendance?

My questions are not designed to embarrass you. They are posed in order to encourage you to question how you planned, organised and conducted each event.

You see it is all too easy for us as directors and managers to fall into the habit of conducting meetings because we have always run meetings. How often do we question whether the meeting should be held at all? How often do we analyse the effectiveness of the meetings we run?

In business there should be no such thing as a *"routine meeting"*. Each meeting should have a defined purpose and if you cannot define your objective(s) then save your company money by cancelling the activity.

Your objectives could include any one or more of the following:

— to impart information

— to modify attitudes

— to make plans

— to solve problems

— to develop a team spirit

— to review performance

— to train

but above all else to agree ACTIONS and achieve IMPROVED RESULTS.

Having defined your objectives the next stage of planning your meeting is the preparation of an AGENDA. This is an aspect of planning which far too many managers either disregard or treat as an afterthought. However, your agenda can and should be a vital document for conditioning the attitudes of your team members towards the meeting.

WHAT ARE THE COMPONENTS OF A MOTIVATIONAL AGENDA?

1. A THEME – these few words should embody the most important objective for the meeting, for example:

   Staying at No 1

   Using the power of persuasive communication

   Offsetting Competitor Activity

   Maximising our potential

2. Each section of the meeting should be introduced in a QUESTIONS format.

   For example:

   How well have we performed as a Company during the first quarter?

   Beneath the main question you could then insert some trigger/prompt words. For example, in the case of the question above:

   — successes

   — disappointments

   — influencing factors

   — lessons learned

   By incorporating questions within the agenda you encourage your team members to PLAN for their attendance at the meeting. The question prompts them to consider the answer. You reinforce this prompting with your covering memo (or e-mail) for example:

   I am enclosing the agenda for next Thursday's quarterly action review meeting. You will see that we will be addressing five key issues, each of which is identified by a question. Please come to the meeting prepared to give your thoughts on, and answers to, the questions raised. I am sure we will have a most productive meeting.

The theme and the questions should create a sense of urgency and importance.

3. The agenda for team meetings should always include reference to a TRAINING SESSION. Bringing your team together enables you to address common training and development issues.

4. Always endeavour to keep the number of subjects/scheduled items within your agenda small. This has a psychological effect on participants. If they receive an agenda with twelve, fifteen or twenty scheduled items the reaction is often:

   How long will this meeting last!

   We'll never get through that lot

   We'll be there all night

5. Incorporate START and FINISH times within the agenda. Your team are then aware of how much time they must allocate for the meeting. When you specify the times make sure you stick to them!

   As you construct your agenda you may fall into another trap. That is the trap of attaching your name to each of the subjects on the agenda. Yes, you are responsible for planning, organising and achieving results from your meetings – but you do not have to conduct every session. DELEGATE the responsibility for planning and conducting some of the sessions to your team members. By giving them the responsibility, authority and accountability you provide them with an opportunity to develop their skill in the following areas:

   — planning a presentation or interactive involvement session

   — controlling an audience

   — questioning

   — handling colleagues reactions/resistances or objections

   — securing action agreements from colleagues

Your aim must be to provide as many of your team members as possible with the opportunity to run a session within your meetings.

Once you have committed yourself to using your meetings to develop your staff there a number of other important issues you need to address. The first is the venue for your meeting.

If training is to form a major part of the meeting then you need to ensure that the meeting room enables you to:

- use the appropriate visual aids, e.g. flipchart, overhead projector, computer and light projector.
- keep the attention of your team. If the room is too small, too large, too dark, too hot, too cold or too noisy then your team will never concentrate on the matters in hand.
- provide comfortable seating and table arrangements. Meetings can often last for many hours and it is essential that all attendees find the seating supportive.

Having selected the appropriate venue for your meeting you need to ensure you conduct the event in a manner which encourages your team to participate to the full.

Here are some guidelines:

- Open the meeting ON TIME. A late start conveys an impression of casualness and a lack of importance to all attendees.
- Open the meeting on a warm, enthusiastic and positive note. When you know your team well there can be an inclination to open the meeting with casual and negative phrases, for example:

  Well here we are again, another review meeting

or

  I know you are all busy so we'll try to get through the agenda in record time

or

  I hope you've all come prepared for today's meeting

- Reaffirm the OBJECTIVES for the meeting.
- Confirm the FORMAT of the meeting.
- Confirm whether you want attendees to take NOTES or whether you are providing HANDOUTS.
- Use VISUAL AIDS wherever possible to support your verbal presentations.
- Ensure the meeting is INTERACTIVE. You develop individuals confidence and competence by involving them as much as you can.

Interaction is achieved by asking STRUCTURED QUESTIONS. The What, How, Who, Where and When prefix ensure that no team member can restrict his or her reply to your questions to just *"yes"* or *"no"*.

— THANK attendees for their positive and constructive contributions. It is so easy to forget the importance of recognition as a motivator of people.

— When PROBLEMS are discussed during your meetings, focus peoples' minds on solutions and not on the identification of a culprit! One of your personnel development tasks is that of ensuring your team members never bring problems to your door without an associated solution or solutions.

— Secure ACTION AGREEMENTS as the meeting progresses and not just at the end of the meeting. Do not advance to the next item on the agenda until the appropriate agreements have been reached and committed to an ACTION PLAN (See Appendix two). It is very common for directors and managers to use MINUTES as their means of recording what was said and what was agreed. On occasions a secretary is called upon to take the minutes and then to produce a word by word document which is subsequently sent to each attendee. In business today the concept of *"minutes"* is totally outdated. Since the objective for all meetings is to achieve agreements and actions then all that attendees need to know is the following:

  — What is to be done

  — How actions are to be completed

  — By whom

  — By when

  — And finally what is to be achieved from completion of the action

Introduce ACTION PLANS at your next team meeting. Delegate responsibility for completing the Action Plan to a member of your team. Complete the document as you progress through the meeting. Photocopy the Action Plan for each delegate at the end of the meeting, or print copies if your team member is using his or her computer for compiling the Action Plan.

Action Plans save you time and they can avoid one of the all too common problems associated with minutes. I am referring to the questions raised (and even disputes stimulated) when the chairman of the meeting reads the minutes of the previous meeting. In meetings individuals can often be heard to say:

I didn't agree to that

or

That wasn't my understanding of that agreement

or

That wasn't the deadline I agreed

The passage of time between the end of a meeting and the issuing of the minutes can lead to attendees developing *"selective memories"*.

SUMMARY

Meetings provide you with the opportunity to lead your team by example. If you plan thoroughly and conduct the meeting in line with my guidelines you will maximise your company's return on the investment made in each meeting.

Refer to Appendix five on page 156 for my *"6P"* approach to business meetings and Checklist six on page 169.

Chapter 20

HOW CONFIDENT ARE YOU WHEN IT COMES TO DEVELOPING YOUR PEOPLE THROUGH FORMAL TRAINING SESSIONS?

As a line manager you fulfil the majority of your training and development responsibilities on a one-to-one basis with your team members. However, when your team share collective training and development requirements the most cost-effective means of addressing these is by means of a group training session.

One-to-one training can, and ideally should, be a relaxed process. However, when it comes to conducting formal training sessions many managers relate to this saying:

> *From the moment we are born our brain functions – until we are asked to give our first formal presentation!*

Do you remember the first time you were asked to *"present"* to a group? How did you feel about the prospect? Did your brain shut down and your stomach go into overdrive?

Be comforted by the fact that 99 out of every 100 people experienced the same feelings as you when they were asked to give their first speech, public talk or presentation. Some of those people still dread the thought of having to *"speak in public"*.

In this chapter you will learn how to develop your formal training and presentation skills.

Like so many aspects of your managerial role, success comes from you believing you CAN achieve. Consider this poem:

If you think you are beaten, you are.
If you think you dare not, you don't.
If you like to win but think you can't
It's almost certain that you won't
Life battles don't always go
To the stronger man and woman
But sooner or later, those who win
Are those who think they can.

How should you plan, organise, conduct and secure positive results from formal presentations and training sessions?

The level of success you achieve from formal training presentations depends heavily upon your PLANNING. As the actress Ruth Gordon said:

> *The best impromptu speeches are written well in advance*

Here are the key factors you should take into account when planning formal presentations and training sessions:

1. What do I want to achieve from giving the presentation/conducting the training session?

   You need to be clear about your objective(s).

2. What is the most appropriate venue for the session?

   Is the meeting room large enough? Is there sufficient seating? Is the seating comfortable? What heating is available? Is air conditioning available? How much natural light enters the room? Does the venue/meeting room have an ambience that is conducive to the subject I will be presenting? How many power points are available? Where are they located? What facility exists to darken the room? (In the event of using a video or computer projector.) Is a flipchart necessary for the presentation? Are there sufficient coloured flipchart pens? Have they run out of ink?

3. What should be incorporated within the agenda for the session?

   Location? Start time? Duration? Break times? Refreshment arrangements? Theme?

4. How will I ensure that my team understands, accepts and actions the training I am proposing to deliver? (Prepare your STRUCTURED QUESTION CHECKLIST)

5. How will my team react to the ideas I am proposing to put forward?

   How will I handle their differing attitudes and reactions?

6. What is the best time to conduct the training session?

   Avoid conducting group training sessions late in the afternoon or on a Friday afternoon. Individuals' receptiveness and ability to assimilate information is greatest early in the day.

7. What presentation style should I employ?

   How can I seek to balance formality and informality during the presentation?

   How appropriate is the introduction of humour within the presentation/discussion?

How can I ensure I display sustained enthusiasm throughout the meeting?

How can I ensure I exclude all negative or unconstructive words and phrases from my presentation?

How can I ensure that the meeting is a "talk with" and not "talk at" session?

How can I ensure that my presentation is structured to be "you", "we" and "us" rather than "I", "me" or "my" orientated?

8. What type of VISUAL AIDS are most appropriate for the presentation/training session?

   When should they be used (consider carefully the SEQUENCE and TIMING)?

   How can I ensure that the visuals I use support my spoken word rather than undermine it?

   What handouts should I issue? In what format should they be produced?

   How important will it be for me to encourage my team members to take notes?

   What audio-visual aids could be used?

   Have I checked on the availability of audio-visual aids?

   Have I checked that these aids work?

   What contingency plans have I prepared in the event of equipment failure?

9. How am I going to OPEN the presentation/training session?

   Should I use:

   Novelty? Intrigue? Humour?

10. How beneficial would it be for me to rehearse aspects of my presentation/training session? Who is the best person to give me feedback on my proposed presentation or training session?

Having planned your presentation or training session by considering carefully the objectives you are seeking to achieve, you can now organise the content to serve your needs and those of your team. I suggest you use my ABC approach to structure your presentation.

ABC refers to:

ATTENTION GRABBER	—	your opening
BODY	—	the heart of your presentation
CLOSE	—	the action commitment stage

The ABC approach follows the principle applied to newscasts of:

— Tell them what you are going to tell them

— Tell them

— Tell them what you told them

HOW SHOULD YOU "OPEN" YOUR PRESENTATION?

Plan your opening and start ON TIME with a warm enthusiastic greeting.

It is important to secure the attention of your audience from the very start of your presentation. Consequently, plan your opening very carefully. Your first THREE sentences will determine whether or not you secure your listener's attention. Practice and develop attention-grabbing statements to open your presentation.

One of the most effective means of generating early audience involvement is by asking each member of the audience a pertinent question.

During your opening confirm to your team that if they have questions on the issues you are presenting to them you want them to raise those questions as and when they come to mind. In addition, advise your team if you expect them to take notes or if you have prepared handouts or other forms of training materials.

HOW SHOULD YOU DEVELOP THE *"BODY"* OF YOUR PRESENTATION?

Because you know your team members you should know what information, and in what form, is likely to be of most interest. You should also know how much detail you need to convey to your team.

Seek to limit the number of points you present in order to maintain clarity.

How should you use visual aids to support your presentations and formal training sessions?

Visual aids should be an essential ingredient of any interactive group presentation or training session for the following reasons:

— They enable you to focus the attention of your audience on specific points.

— They help you to control the presentation.

— They give your presentation a structure and act as a prompt.

— They help people to remember the more important points of your presentation.

— They make your presentation more interesting.

— Well-prepared and effectively used visual aids convey an impression of professionalism to your audience.

— They enable difficult points to be explained and understood more easily.

— They reinforce your verbal messages.

However, remember that visual aids should be just that – visual aids. You as the speaker have the responsibility to express your ideas to your listeners, then reinforce them where appropriate, with a visual.

Good visual aids clarify, unify or emphasise ideas – they do not compete with them or you.

WHAT GUIDELINES SHOULD YOU FOLLOW WHEN YOU USE VISUAL AID EQUIPMENT?

1. FLIP CHARTS

Always leave a blank sheet between each prepared flip chart. This allows you to control the attention of your group, and you can remove one visual without revealing the contents of the next until you are ready. In addition, it provides space to expand on, or explain points which arise during the presentation.

Write sufficiently largely and legibly to enable the group to read your text without problems. Use colours for emphasis, but do not use too many on a single page.

Do not put too much detail on each sheet. Use bullet points and then you can enlarge verbally on each one.

Use techniques to enhance your effectiveness. As an example, the text on the flip chart might read … THIS PRODUCES A REDUCTION OF … per cent.

You should write the percentage you wish to insert, in soft pencil, in the margin of the sheet, in tiny figures. You can see it, your audience cannot. Then fill in the apparently missing information at the desired times.

2. PROMPT (CUE) CARDS

Use prompt cards, sequentially numbered, which contain the key outlines of your presentation. The cards also instruct you when to use the flip chart or any other visual. For example:

(i) *How can we achieve …?* (Visual 1)*

(ii) *From this we can see that …* (Visual 2 – write example and issue Handout A)

(iii) *What should be our proposed plan of action?* (Visual 3)

*Use a different colour for your prompt notes on visuals.

However, do not hold on to your cards, otherwise they can be viewed by your audience as crutches rather than prompts. Holding the cards can also lead to you losing eye contact with your audience.

3. WHITE BOARDS

Always start with a clean board otherwise the remaining contents can be a distraction to your team.

Write or print so that everybody in the room can read your message easily.

When talking, face the audience, not the board.

Remember, you will rarely, if ever, over-use a board.

4. OVERHEAD PROJECTOR

Refer to my recommendations on using flip charts when you are proposing to use prepared acetates.

When you use prepared acetates, it is useful to have a piece of paper/card to cover up parts of your text, which you can reveal when appropriate. Remember to place the paper *under* the acetate. The weight of the acetate will help to stop the paper falling from the Overhead Projector.

When using TYPED acetates ensure that the type size is at least three times that of the size used in normal correspondence. Do not use all upper case text for your acetates, since it can be difficult for your audience to read.

Turn off the projector, or cover it with your reveal sheet, when you will be talking for more than a few sentences between visuals. If your projector remains on this can be another source of distraction.

When a pointer is necessary, use it and put it down immediately to avoid distracting the audience. Alternatively, rest the pointer on the reflecting plate of the OHP.

When using a large OHP ensure you place it on a low table or trolley in order to avoid the mirror stem blocking your audiences' view.

Always check to ensure your acetates do not contain any spelling mistakes.

5. 35MM SLIDES AND MULTIMEDIA

Place the remote control or mouse to a flat surface, so your hands are free to move naturally.

When using a remote control, use a colour code so you know which button "advances" slides and which goes in reverse.

Although the room may be dark, look towards your audience and stay animated so your voice remains interesting.

When using computers (desk or lap top) ensure that people have a clear view of the screen. Always check that your screen can be read if members of your audience are sitting to the side of the screen.

6. HANDOUTS

Handouts can serve two basic functions:

— they supplement your presentations

— they act as a working document

When supplementing your presentation they are best distributed at the end of the meeting. This kind of handout is often a hard copy of your visuals or additional data.

When you use a handout as a working document try to keep people from flipping ahead by:

— explaining the purpose of the handout and how you will use it

— (where appropriate) dividing the handout into sections and discussing them in turn

Remember, handouts can be *"silent salesmen"* after your presentation, so ensure they are simple, clear, brief and above all convey *"benefits"* to the recipient.

Ensure your handouts do not contain spelling mistakes.

HOW CAN YOU ENHANCE YOUR PRESENTATION TECHNIQUES?

We have looked at WHAT you are going to present and visual methods of supporting your message.

However, it is probably true to say that despite the most exhaustive and in-depth preparation, if you cannot deliver your message effectively, the presentation or training session will be unlikely to achieve its aim.

"Nerves" are the biggest problem for most speakers, and presentation skills involve the productive use of nervous energy. Therefore, regardless of the format of your presentation, the following guidelines will help you make the best use of your presentation skills:

1. MAINTAIN EYE CONTACT WITH YOUR LISTENERS

— Do not move your gaze from the floor to the ceiling via the wall. Look at the people, not aggressively or hypnotically, just look at them as you do in normal conversation. That means all of your group, including those at the sides.

— Finish a phrase or a thought with one person, then move to another. But do not apply a searchlight sweep.

— Pause when you check your notes and talk only when you have established eye contact.

— Maintaining eye contact will help you to:

  — build credibility with your audience

  — gauge listeners' reactions to your ideas

  — keep each person involved

  — finish sentences strongly (do not let your voice drop at the end of a sentence)

— If you have a large group, mentally divide the audience into sections and make eye contact with one person in each section of the audience. The others in the area will feel they are included. Use a different person as your contact each time you return to a section.

— Do not hold your notes when you are presenting. Place them on the table and angle them towards you by placing a support under the notes.

2. PROJECT AND ANIMATE YOUR VOICE

Your voice is the most natural aid you have, but it can be made ineffective by:

— MUMBLING – it is better to be too loud than too quiet.

— HESITANCY – excessive pauses, usually filled with "er", "um" are almost always a sign of insufficient rehearsal.

— GABBLING – speaking too quickly and indistinctly. I often refer to this as "the verbal speed wobble!"

— CATCH PHRASES – such as "at this point in time", "and all that sort of thing", "you know what I mean". Whilst harmless in themselves, if they are too frequent they can distract and irritate your audience.

— DROPPING YOUR VOICE – particularly at the end of each sentence. It becomes very tedious, since it makes it appear the presentation has ended with each sentence and has to be started off again each time.

Retain your natural accent. Because you are conducting a formal session you do not have to develop an over-formal or even pompous tone of voice.

Vary your pitch. Light and shade is what will hold your audience's attention.

Show enthusiasm through your voice, and emotion too, where appropriate. Remember that the tone of your voice is conditioned by your feelings, empathy and sincerity towards the subject you are communicating.

Use pace for emphasis, but slow down when giving facts and figures.

3. KEEP YOUR HANDS FREE TO GESTURE

- Avoid pockets, pens and your other hand. When your hands are unencumbered, you do not need to think about gestures, they come naturally.
- Gestures allow you to:
  - be your own best visual aid
  - reinforce key points
  - keep your voice range moving
  - marshall all your energy to explain your ideas
  - direct your audience's attention
- However, when you are *"speaking with your hands"* there are positions you should avoid.

  Avoid placing your hands on your hips. It can convey the impression of being condescending or of being parental i.e. *"You're in trouble now"*.

  Avoid crossing your hands in front of you. It can indicate weakness or timidity.

  Avoid *"standing at ease on parade"*. With your hands behind your back and body rigid you can give the impression of either having no energy or of being disinterested.

  Avoid having your hands in your pockets. This can convey disinterest or nervousness and it can be a distraction to your team members.

4. PAUSE TO EMPHASISE POINTS

- Give yourself thinking time and allow your listeners to absorb what you have said.

  Far too many managers consider that if they pause during a presentation then they will lose control or the impetus will be lost. Rarely is either the result.

  Pauses always seem longer to the presenter than to an audience. Your audience has to reflect upon, and comprehend, what you have said. This takes time.

Whenever you feel concerned about the introduction of pauses within your training sessions and presentations remember this saying:

Treat silence as an ally and not an enemy

5. USE NATURAL MOVEMENTS TO REINFORCE YOUR IDEAS

Controlled and carefully considered movement animates your presentation.

Remember your team are not listening to a tape. They expect you to be enthusiastic, excited, interested and outgoing and your words alone will not convey each of these characteristics.

Your movement has to be timed and its nature related to the point you are seeking to convey. If you pace up and down aimlessly, swivel in your chair, or use excessive physical gestures then your audience will be distracted and your message will not be delivered successfully.

When you are conducting a formal training session for your team ensure you present your subject matter while STANDING. If you sit down you will be restricted in the number and type of movements you can convey. Sitting can also convey the impression that the subject you are presenting is of limited importance.

6. POINTERS TO EVEN MORE SUCCESSFUL PRESENTATIONS AND FORMAL TRAINING SESSIONS

Personality plays a very important part in presentations, but do not fall into the trap of self-glorification. Present the subject, not yourself. CONCENTRATE MORE OF YOUR ATTENTION ON INFORMING RATHER THAN PERFORMING.

Nerves are important to all successful speakers. They indicate your concern about the quality of your presentation, and that you have not become over-confident. If you feel nervousness building up, it helps to breath deeply, to slow down the pace of your presentation, and to smile.

Smiling is such a simple act and yet so few managers seem to be able to do it when they are running meetings, giving presentations or training sessions. A smile, genuinely expressed, relaxes your audience and creates warmth.

Talk with people and not down to them.

The formality of a presentation should not lead to a situation where you appear to be autocratic or domineering. Make your group sessions INTERACTIVE. Get people involved. If your sessions are *"talk at"* rather than *"talk with"* in style you will never know how successful they have been. Interaction ensures you are aware of your audience's attitudes towards the subject(s) you are presenting.

Use humour sparingly.

Some managers think that jokes or sarcasm relax an audience. Sarcasm rarely does and jokes often fall flat. Few of us have the ability to convey humour spontaneously and we can never be absolutely certain that what seems funny to us will be funny to our audience.

I would recommend that you err on the side of caution... *"When in doubt leave humour out"*.

Your formal presentations and training sessions should spark interest and involvement. As a consequence you may stimulate individuals to raise difficult or negative issues. Do not seek to avoid these, use my Accept Agree and Capitalise approach wherever possible. The AAC© approach is described in Chapter sixteen.

I have already referred to the importance of standing when you are presenting to groups. However, when you want to get into discussion with your team members sit down. By sitting you are conveying your desire to get involved in, or listen to, the discussion. Sitting also relaxes your audience and removes the *"authority figure"* you conveyed while standing.

Holding the attention and interest of your team is always helped when you structure your presentation to be *"you"*, *"we"* and *"us"* orientated, rather than *"me"*, *"my"* and *"I"*.

Let me illustrate with the following example. A Production Manager is running a training session for a group of his engineers on new safety techniques and he has fallen into the *"Me"*, *"My"* and *"I"* trap:

> *I wanted to get you all together today to discuss what I consider to be some very important developments in factory safety procedures. It has always been my view that safety has to be my main concern as Production Manager.*

If he continues in that vein then his team is likely to be less than enthusiastic towards the new procedures. However, suppose his style was to change as follows:

> *Over the last three years each of you have demonstrated the importance you place on safety within the factory. Your efforts have resulted in a substantial drop in accidents. It is because of your interest and concern that I wanted to introduce you to a number of exciting new approaches which will enhance our safety record further still.*

The Production Manager has switched to the *"you"*, *"we"* and *"our"* approach and his chances of winning his team's support for his ideas will have increased substantially.

Beware of quoting your OPINIONS during presentations or training sessions. Support your recommendations with evidence of success. All managers are tempted, at some time, to voice their opinion during presentations. But your audience could be thinking, and may even express, the following:

> *You would say that, wouldn't you?*

When you are presenting to your team members you may (unwittingly) fall into the trap of SPEAKING BEFORE YOU THINK. On such occasions you may express, what I refer to as CASUAL PHRASES. These are the remarks we often live to regret and which we cannot excuse. Here are some examples:

> *This idea has had some success and hopefully, it will work for you* (and maybe it will not)
>
> *It's an idiot proof system* (who's calling me an idiot!)
>
> *To be honest* (so other things you have said have been dishonest?)
>
> *This may be confusing* (why?)
>
> *I'm not sure if this will appeal to you* (if you are not sure then why are you presenting it?)
>
> *Obviously you can see …* (it may be obvious to you, but not to me)

Familiarity with your audience may help you to relax – but always make a conscious and sustained effort to choose your words and phrases with great care. One casual remark could destroy the impact of your presentation.

HOW EFFECTIVELY DO YOU PROMOTE DISCUSSION AND HANDLE QUESTIONS DURING FORMAL TRAINING SESSIONS AND BUSINESS PRESENTATIONS?

People will be more likely to understand, agree with and remember your ideas when they participate in the meeting. It is an effective means of meeting your objectives and reducing the time needed to persuade others. So how is involvement achieved?

STRUCTURED QUESTIONING IS THE KEY TO INTERACTIVE PRESENTATIONS

When planning each of your presentations you should consider the nature and extent of the questions your audience may ask:

— Analyse your listeners' background, needs and concerns.

— List the questions your presentation is likely to generate and prepare and rehearse answers.

The table below shows typical categories of questions and the possible motives of the questioner.

CATEGORY OF QUESTION	THE POSSIBLE MOTIVES OF YOUR QUESTIONER	MY SUGGESTED APPROACH
Sincere	He or she missed or misinterpreted what was said.	Acknowledge and, if necessary, repeat your question (it gives you time to think).
	He or she needs more information.	If there has been a misunderstanding be careful how you indicate this.
	He or she honestly disagrees on a point.	Answer factually and honestly.
Conversational	He or she needs to establish a presence at every meeting.	You must interject politely and firmly and seek to clarify a specific question or concern they wish to raise.
	He or she has something to say on every subject.	
	He or she finds a release from tension by joking or switching subjects.	The use of a person's name can be of great help when you seek to gain support for your ideas.
Supportive	He or she wants to emphasise one of your points.	Always acknowledge your supporter by name.
	He or she wants to get you out of trouble by changing the subject.	Keep your comments brief and general e.g. *"Thank you Brian for that view."*
	He or she wants to help you to change the pace or direction of the meeting.	Respond positively to the suggestion e.g. *"Let's look now at."*
Hostile	He or she likes to test everyone.	Restate the question, but rephrase it in order to be positive. Do not respond defensively – this could provoke further hostility.
	He or she disagrees with anything you say.	
	He or she is attacking another subject in this question.	
	He or she resents your content or style.	

When you are responding to your audience's questions you will find it helpful to follow my BUIC© approach.

BUIC is my acronym for:

BREVITY	You will find that the best answer is always the short answer.
UNDERSTANDING	You should acknowledge all questions objectively – never insult a questioner no matter how unimportant or frivolous you consider the question.
INFORMATION	You may need to provide additional details about a particular point, or clarify what has already been said.
CONVICTION	Your audience wants to know that you believe what you are saying.

How can you generate interaction (discussion and debate) during your presentations and formal training sessions?

The formality of a group meeting can discourage some attendees from raising questions. They can feel nervous or self-conscious and some individuals are inclined to leave others to raise questions.

You want each person to benefit from the session you are conducting and that necessitates you using techniques to ensure they are all involved.

At the beginning of each formal meeting presentation or training session state that you want each person to raise their questions, concerns or reservations as these arise in their minds.

As you conclude each section of your presentation ask individuals structured questions which can identify any one or more of the following:

— their ATTITUDES

— their UNDERSTANDING

— their ACCEPTANCE of the points conveyed

— their willingness to ACT upon your presentation/training

Ensure you never use the following unstructured questions:

Has anyone any questions?

or

Does anyone want to ask a question?

Both questions are likely to produce a stony silence.

WHAT ARE SOME OF THE MOST COMMON PITFALLS TO AVOID WHEN CONDUCTING GROUP PRESENTATIONS?

In order to succeed when making group presentations, it is important to be aware of the many traps which await the inexperienced presenter.

Here are some of the most common:

1. LACK OF CLARITY

You must avoid talking *"over the heads"* of your group. During every presentation, it is essential you ask specific questions to confirm that your audience has understood fully your key points.

2. LACK OF CONFIDENCE

This is most easily recognised by your audience when you use such words as:

> *If, Hopefully, Perhaps* or *Maybe*.

The deletion of these words from your presentations will be achieved if you always think before your speak.

3. LACK OF ATTENTION TO DETAIL

One of the most common complaints of managers is that they *"never have enough time"*. Sadly the remark is expressed most often by those managers who are seeking to justify or excuse their lack of planning and attention to detail.

Well I need to remind you that you do have enough time. In fact, you have all there is, you will never get any more.

In order for you to be both EFFICIENT (doing the job right) and EFFECTIVE (doing the right job) you must pay attention to detail.

Budget time to plan your presentations and training sessions. Protect that time. Remember you will only have one chance to get your points across to your audience in a manner they will understand, accept and action.

SUMMARY

Formal presentations and training sessions are a very important means of developing your people to develop your company. Approach them with confidence and enjoy the buzz of stimulating your team members to grow as a group.

Chapter 21

ROLE-PLAYS – HOW TO ENABLE YOUR TEAM MEMBERS TO PRACTICE AND MASTER THE TECHNIQUES YOU HAVE INTRODUCED

Do you recall the old saying............ *"PRACTICE MAKES PERFECT"*.

I am sure you do and you have probably expressed it on at least one occasion to your team members. However, have you ever examined and questioned the validity of the saying? If you have you will have realised that the saying is fundamentally flawed. If you practice something over and over again which you do not undertake correctly then all that results is a situation where you are simply increasing the number of occasions on which you make mistakes.

But suppose I amend the saying as follows ...*"Practice and ANALYSIS helps to make you perfect"*.

Of course I have still not defined what is meant by the term *"perfect"*, but the insertion of the word *"analysis"* has made the saying more relevant. Your personnel development role requires you to PRACTICE your team members and ANALYSE their performance. One of the means of achieving these goals is ROLE-PLAY activities.

This chapter describes how you can ensure role-play activity helps you to develop your personnel.

Role-playing can be defined as follows:

> *Practising, under simulated, but structured conditions, techniques which are designed to improve an individual's performance.*

Role-play bridges the gap between formal training sessions, where people acquire new knowledge, and on-the-job training. Role-playing is NOT play-acting. It is designed to closely reflect (within the limits of the training room) the work environment.

Role-play sessions can be structured to allow individuals to:

— push against their "comfort zone" in a low-risk environment

— demonstrate specific techniques

— react spontaneously to situations

— analyse their own strengths and shortcomings

— explore single or multiple situations and problems

As a training method, role-playing offers a number of benefits:

1. It makes an individual self-conscious.

   This is desirable since you, as the trainer, want your team member to become aware of his or her strengths and shortcomings.

   It is a common occurrence when role playing that a person makes the same mistakes he or she has been making unconsciously while undertaking his or her job.

2. It stimulates an exchange of views and opinions amongst a group on such areas as *"style"*, *"method"*, *"technique"*, *"mannerisms"* and *"reactions"* to the approach adopted by the main participant in the role-play. The discussion helps the role player to obtain a better insight to the effects of his or her actions and words on others.

3. It encourages the exchange of knowledge.

4. It can reveal attitudes, perceptions and prejudices.

5. It has the advantage of emphasising SHOWING how to do or say something rather than TELLING how to do or say it.

6. It provides an environment in which individuals can experiment with techniques without the fear of the live consequences.

7. For the person enacting the role of the recipient in the role-play, it allows him or her to experience (perhaps for the first time) the differences between the two participants of the situation.

Each of the benefits shown above can be lost if role-play sessions are not conducted in the right way. Here are my guidelines for planning, organising and conducting role-play activities.

The majority of people have a reluctance to *"perform"* in front of their colleagues. Therefore, it is important to explain to all participants the following:

— The role-play is not an academic exercise, since it will be concerned with REAL business situations.

— You recognise that the role play cannot simulate every aspect of the real event and, therefore, this will be taken into account during the post role-play analysis.

— That individuals will be given adequate time to plan their role-play.

— That the person who is the recipient of the role-play will be working to a brief prepared by the role-player.

— That the role-play will take place away from other members of the team – ideally, in another room where it will be recorded on CCTV for analysis purposes. The remaining members of the team would view the role-play live on a television in an adjacent or linked room/office.

— The role-player is NOT the person who is *"in the spotlight"*. The main attention should be on the observers. They are the ones who will be providing constructive feedback. If they cannot recognise the strengths and shortcomings of their colleague then they will miss these qualities and characteristics in themselves.

— The recording of a role-play on CCTV aids analysis.

— All members of the audience to a role-play will be invited to provide feedback. The role-player will also be asked to comment on the observer's analysis.

The observers of a role-play are there to provide EFFECTIVE feedback. By this term I mean that all feedback should be:

SPECIFIC	Comments such as "that was quite good" or "that wasn't good enough" do not provide the participant in the role-play with anything meaningful on which to take action.
CONSTRUCTIVE	Criticism on its own serves no purpose.
POSITIVE	Everyone likes to know what they have done well. This is not praise for the sake of praise. Very often individuals do not recognise their strengths and, as a consequence, do not capitalise to the full on their ability.

If observers express criticisms then they must be able to demonstrate HOW the action should have been undertaken. When role-plays are well planned, organised and conducted, every member of your team will benefit from the activity. Individuals will develop and will recognise the progress they are making.

Refer to Checklist seven and seven/1 on pages 171 and 174 for my Manager's Guide to Training Methods and the Training Cycle.

Refer to Checklist twelve and thirteen on pages 180 and 182 for two Role-Play Assessment methods.

CHAPTER 22

DELEGATION – ONE OF YOUR MOST IMPORTANT MEANS OF DEVELOPING YOUR STAFF

Ask any director or manager if he delegates and the prompt reply is likely to be, *"of course I do"*. Yet managers often confuse delegation with either abdication or the giving out of tasks.

This chapter explains the nature of delegation and how to use it to develop your staff.

DELEGATION can be defined as:

> *Giving another person AUTHORITY to act on your behalf, for a prescribed period of time, by making him or her RESPONSIBLE for seeing that the task is done and holding him or her ACCOUNTABLE for the results.*

You might notice that the words AUTHORITY, RESPONSIBLE and ACCOUNTABLE have been highlighted.

AUTHORITY means giving the right or power to make decisions and to take actions. When you give another person the authority to act on your behalf, then you are bound by the decision(s) he or she makes.

RESPONSIBILITY means giving an individual ownership and understanding of the task or job you are asking him or her to undertake.

ACCOUNTABILITY means requiring the individual to whom the task has been delegated to take the credit or criticism for the outcome of his actions. To quote the late American President Truman *"the buck stops here"*.

The definition also refers to delegation as the assignment of a task for a *"prescribed period of time"*. By its very nature delegation is a temporary assignment. If you assign the task on a permanent basis then it would no longer be part of your job, but an addition to one of your team member's jobs.

How does delegation differ from *"abdication"* or the *"giving out of jobs"*?

Abdication can be defined as:

> *The action of formally disowning and the surrender of ownership*

It occurs when a manager does one of the following:

— walks away from a task, in the hope that someone within his team will take on the task

or

— thinks he has delegated a task to a team member but when doing so leaves that person to get on with it, unaided, untrained and with no support or encouragement

or

— hands over a piece of work to one of his staff and then disowns it, including his own accountability for the result

Giving out jobs is something every manager does every day. It concerns the ROUTINE aspects of a manager's job – many of which the manager's staff are all too familiar with. The act of giving out jobs does little, if anything to develop staff.

Before considering HOW delegation should be undertaken it is useful to reflect upon WHY so many managers find it hard to delegate.

There are a number of reasons, including:

— A natural reluctance on the part of managers to release their responsibilities to others.

— Some managers maintain that they can always do things better or faster than their team members can.

— Some managers fear that if they give additional responsibilities to a team member that individual's performance may reflect unfavourably on themselves.

— A few managers cannot be bothered to train their staff to take on new responsibilities.

— Most managers like to be seen to be busy. They think that delegation will lead to them having *"time on their hands"*.

But the benefits to be gained from delegation far outweigh the concerns of managers.

Here are seven key reasons for making delegation a matter of importance to you as a manager:

1. No manager can develop his or her own knowledge and skills if he or she is not delegating. Without delegation managers can become *"busy fools"* preoccupied with matters of the moment and consumed with *"getting things done"*.

2. If you do not practice delegation then the amount of time you spend at work is likely to increase and the only thing you are likely to gain from working fifteen or sixteen hours a day is ulcers.

3. You need to utilise all the skills of your team members. They need to develop and grow in their jobs. They need to be given opportunities to think and decide on important matters for themselves. Delegation accelerates an individual's learning curve and reduces his boredom curve.

4. Delegation gives you time to plan and think. As managers advance their careers they need to acknowledge that the physical activity that was a characteristic of their junior roles is replaced steadily by mental activity.

5. Delegation helps you to increase your productivity. By delegating tasks to your staff you are able to [illegible] activities which should benefit your company.

6. Delegation can motivate the individuals who take on new tasks and it develops their sense of responsibility. Remember, if you let go, people will grow.

7. Management is essentially *"achieving results through others"*. Therefore, if you do not delegate you will become a *"doer"* an individual who supervises but one who does not manage.

Once you are committed to using delegation as a means of developing your team follow the guidelines shown below:

1. Review each of the activities you undertake when carrying out your job. Identify those you could delegate to your team members.

2. Once you have selected the tasks determine:

   — the result(s) you want to achieve from the delegation

   — who would be the best person to carry out the task (attitude and aptitude)

   — what actions you will have to fulfil to complete the delegation

3. Discuss the task you wish to delegate with the person you would like to take on the responsibility. Establish if he or she wants to accept the delegated task. Remember delegation is not coercive in nature. Individuals should want to accept additional responsibilities.

4. Agree with your team member the following:

   — what you both expect to achieve from the delegation (clear, specific and measurable objectives)

   — the time limits and deadlines

- — the individual's limits of authority
- — the resources he or she needs to fulfil the task
- — the training he or she needs to complete the task successfully
- — how you will monitor his or her progress

5. Notify those people within your company/organisation who need to be aware of your team member's additional temporary responsibility.
6. Do NOT work out the detail of HOW you consider your team member should fulfil the task. If you do you are not delegating, you are just giving out work. Delegation should encourage your team member to think for him/herself and to make his or her own decisions.

All delegation is built on a FOUNDATION OF TRUST. Study the two illustrations below and on the next page to see the results of DISTRUST and TRUST.

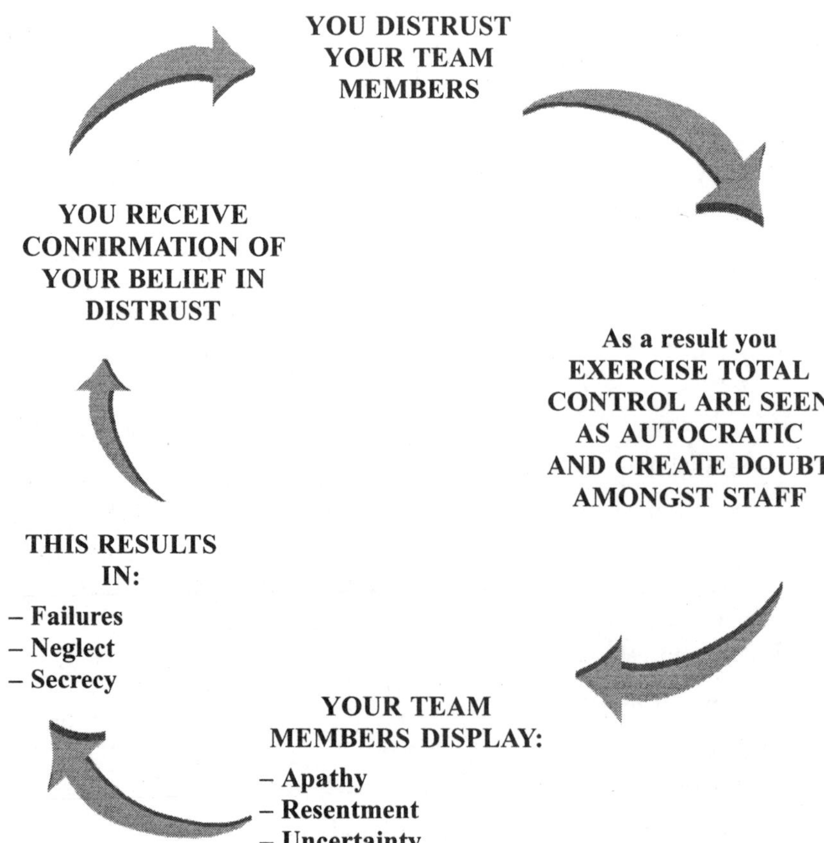

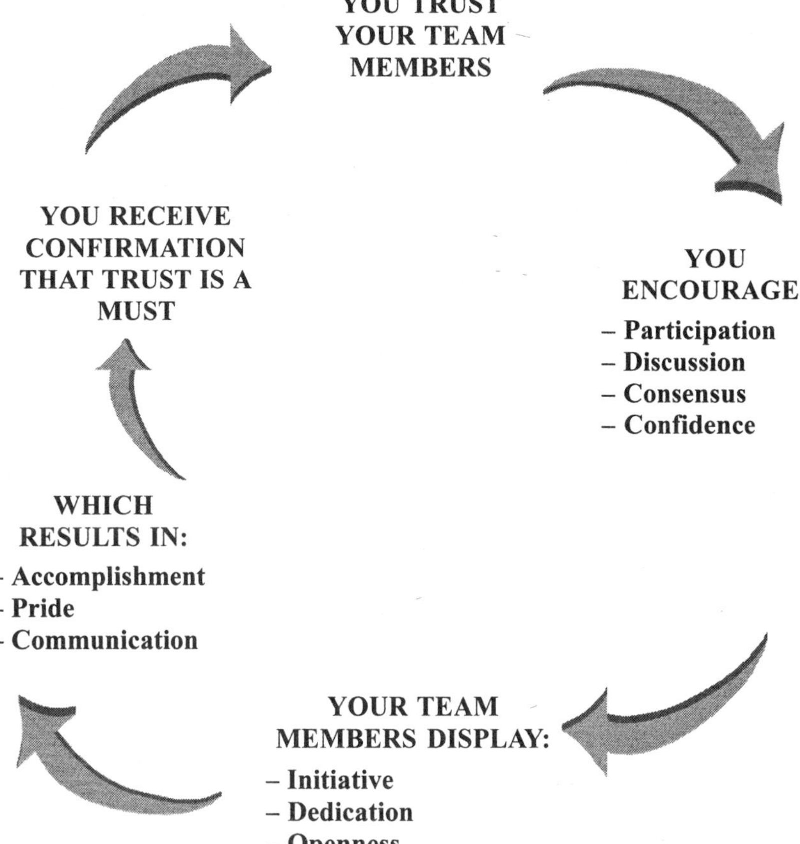

SUMMARY

Your success as a delegator will never be measured by how, to whom and how often you delegate. You will be judged by the results you achieve.

Delegation is an act of faith as it involves risk – the risk of failure. Remember you remain fully accountable for the task.

It is not easy to give people the right to be wrong, when you will be accountable for the mistakes that are made.

However, the long-term benefits far outweigh the short-term pain. Good managers delegate effectively. Do you?

Refer to Checklist eight on page 175 to learn how you can evaluate whether you are delegating effectively.

CHAPTER 23

DEVELOPING YOUR TEAM MEMBERS THROUGH COACHING AND COUNSELLING

Every time you communicate with your team members you have the opportunity to influence the attitudes of each person. Therefore, you need to give careful consideration to your wording and your tone of voice when you communicate. This is particularly important when you are involved in COACHING and COUNSELLING your team members.

COACHING is the process of providing informal guidance, encouragement, advice and feedback to an individual. COUNSELLING involves you in the discussion of both personal and professional issues with a team member.

This chapter will introduce you to techniques that will help you to develop your coaching and counselling skills and, thereby, develop the abilities of your staff and the results of your company.

Let's consider the subject of COACHING first. Successful coaches work hard at understanding their team members. How they feel, think and react. Without such knowledge they cannot tailor their communication. Tailoring is not just about what is said, but about how, when and where communication takes place.

Effective coaches know that when things are going well for their team members the word *"YES"* needs to feature strongly in their (the Coach's) vocabulary. The word *"YES"* acts as a positive reinforcement of success. Here are some examples:

> *Yes, that really went well for you*
>
> *Yes, that was a difficult situation, which you tackled with great confidence*
>
> *Yes, you really have got the hang of that process*

When things are not going as well as a good coach would wish he uses SILENCE and provides EFFECTIVE FEEDBACK. I have used the word EFFECTIVE to highlight the fact that successful coaches provide feedback through DISCUSSION and not TELLING.

Discussion incorporates the following positive features:

— it is a two-way communication process

— it encourages initiative and self management

— it encourages individuals to give commitments

— it encourages individuals to analyse their own performance

Telling, on the other hand, has the following negative features:

— it is a one-way communication process

— it encourages a dependence upon the TELLER

— it can often result in employee resentment and resistance

— it promotes assumptions or pretensions of understanding

— it encourages the recipient of the telling to stop listening

Ineffective coaches are tellers and not discussers. They use a different language. When things are going wrong the coach uses the word *"NO"* frequently and he introduces some form of rebuke, correction or punishment. As a consequence, employees are inclined to:

— criticise their manager and often their company

— work in isolation

— compete destructively against colleagues

— work erratically, ineffectively and only under coersion

— make excuses

— and defend themselves

Develop your people by building *"YES"* into your coaching vocabulary. Focus on an individual's strengths and successes. Support and respect your team members.

To enhance your coaching ability I would like to offer some guidelines on how to give your team members encouragement and positive feedback on their performances.

1. Always make your feedback refer to ONE SPECIFIC PERFORMANCE.

   Generalised compliments such as *"You're doing a great job"* can be seen as lacking in substance or even false. If this occurs your credibility can be damaged.

2. Keep your encouragement PURE – do not confuse the message with anything else.

   When you mix encouragement with advice it causes people not to believe in your compliment. Here are two examples of this lack of purity:

   > *Bill, you handled the Reynolds Project both quickly and with great enthusiasm. However, with another project of that sort make certain you keep all the other Departmental Heads informed of your progress.*

   and

   > *Sue, you really handled that difficult customer with coolness and tact. But make certain that when you meet someone like that again you take more notes of his or her comments.*

3. Make your feedback on good performances always POSITIVE in nature. Use silence and invite your team member to analyse the outcome of a poor performance.

   By reminding your team member of his or her good performance you will encourage the consistency of good work habits.

4. Offer encouragement IMMEDIATELY AFTER the performance has taken place.

   When you give feedback soon after the desired or successful performance you motivate and reinforce your messages.

5. Once a performance level has been reached do not continue to compliment your team member on repeating the performance.

   Your aim is to develop individuals' confidence and competence. You should be encouraging them to move to the next performance level and not to settle for a comfort level.

Whilst it might be wonderful if our managerial life comprised solely of giving positive feedback and encouragement life is just not like that. Instead we are called upon to offer advice and to counsel our staff.

By giving people advice you can change the quality and quantity of their performance – the way they do something and the frequency of that action. In order to ensure your advice is accepted and used follow these guidelines:

1. When you are advising someone to change his or her current performance describe the nature of that performance SPECIFICALLY.

If your description is vague and ill-defined your team member will not necessarily understand what you want him or her to change. Shown below are two examples of ill-defined descriptions of current performance:

To a salesman:

> *You know Bill you will have to be better at opening new accounts.*

To a production worker:

> *Steve, you need to up your productivity.*

Here are descriptions in far more specific terms:

To the salesman:

> *Bill, your current ratio of new accounts opened to prospective customer calls made is 1 in 12.*

To the production worker:

> *Steve, you are currently producing six units each hour.*

2. State SPECIFICALLY the change or different result you want from your team member.

   For the examples shown above the changes could be:

   > *Bill, working with you I want to help you to reduce your current ratio to 1 in 6 within 3 months.*

   > *Steve, by adopting two new approaches, which I will describe, you will be able to increase your productivity to nine units each hour.*

3. Keep your advice PURE.

   Do not try to soften it with compliments or distracting discussion, because if you mix encouragement and advice people are inclined to question your sincerity and the need to follow your advice.

4. Offer advice JUST BEFORE your team member has an opportunity to use it.

   If your advice is offered in isolation of the opportunity to use it, then the passage of time may ensure your team member either forgets the content of the advice or the context in which it should be used.

5. LIMIT THE SCOPE of your advice.

   Try to address one key issue at a time. This will help to ensure the advice is taken.

6. INVITE YOUR TEAM MEMBER TO DISCUSS YOUR ADVICE.

   You need to ensure your team member understands, accepts and will apply your advice. Use probe questions such as ... *"What are your views on ...?", "What is your attitude towards ...?"* and *"What is your opinion of ...?"*

Let me turn now to the role COUNSELLING has to play in the development of your staff.

Earlier I mentioned that counselling can be of a personal or professional nature. It is not my intention in this book to address the complex area of personal counselling. Instead I want to focus on issues related to counselling staff on professional matters, those that relate directly to employees jobs.

All personnel development starts with ensuring individuals attitudes are positive and most counselling begins by addressing an individual's attitudes.

At this point let me draw a distinction between counselling and corrective discussions. The former is concerned primarily with the prevention of problems, whereas corrective discussions occur when something has gone wrong, sometimes after, and in spite of, counselling.

During your managerial career you could be called upon to counsel team members on a hundred and one different issues relating to their jobs. However, regardless of the subject your discussions should be constructed around the sequence shown below and overleaf:

PLANNING THE DISCUSSION
(Timing, venue, format, duration, style and objective)

↓

OPENING THE DISCUSSION
(Putting your team member at ease/setting the scene)

↓

STRUCTURED QUESTIONING
(To enable your team member to recognise and acknowledge his or her need to address the subject under discussion)

↓

INVITE YOUR TEAM MEMBER TO PROPOSE

A COURSE OF ACTION
(This gives the individual ownership of the matter)

↓

AGREEING A COURSE OF ACTION
(Commit this to paper and include a review procedure within the course of action)

Of course at any time during the counselling session you may be called upon to handle the resistances, concerns or objections of your team member.

Successful counselling can make a significant contribution to the development of staff. But that success is dependent upon a variety of matters relating to the framework above.

You cannot counsel someone on a work-related issue unless you have planned it in detail. Some managers think they can *"wing it"*. This American expression means to undertake the activity without any planning. Well if you elect to take this approach be assured you will not get off the runway!

Let's look at some of the key elements of planning a counselling discussion:

1. TIMING

Never try to counsel someone at the end of the working day or week. As they wind down for the day or week they are rarely in a receptive mood for what may be a long discussion.

Seek to hold counselling sessions early in the week and early in the day. Then you will be able to provide your team member with immediate support.

Do not schedule a counselling session until you have identified what other demands your team member may have on his or her time.

Schedule your discussion no more than 48 hours in advance and ideally within the forthcoming 24 hours. When appointments are arranged far in advance employees can allow their minds to wander and to imagine all manner of negative thoughts.

Hold your discussion on time. If you are late you can convey the impression to your team member that you do not consider the meeting to be important.

2. VENUE

You will be discussing an issue related to your team member's job and therefore, you may be tempted to conduct that discussion in the workplace. Consider whether an external venue may be more conducive for the discussions.

Ensure your chosen venue offers you privacy and freedom from interruption. I never cease to be amazed at the number of occasions on which I have sat in a hotel reception or lounge area and overheard managers counselling, correcting or even disciplining staff. Do they really believe they will achieve their objective in a setting that can best be described as a public goldfish bowl!

3. DURATION

Consider carefully how much time you believe you will need for your discussions – and then budget double that time. Counselling stimulates emotions and, as a consequence, discussions often take far longer than managers anticipate. Your team member should not feel under a time pressure. Therefore avoid the following:

— commenting to your team member that ... *"We better get through this quickly – because I've got a lot to do today" or "This will not take long – because I've got a meeting at ... "*

— frequently checking the time on your watch

— dropping casual phrases into the discussion, such as ... *"Time's pressing, let's get on"* or *"Come on, we can't discuss this all night"*

4. STYLE AND FORMAT

Successful counsellors know that bringing about a change in an employee's behaviour and, as a consequence, performance is achieved most successfully when the employee recognises that he or she has a NEED to change. Bringing about the recognition is achieved through STRUCTURED QUESTIONING. Therefore, plan the questions you wish to ask your team member in order to enable him or her to recognise the need for change. Plan to ask the questions in a relaxed and conversational style.

5. OBJECTIVE SETTING

If you do not have a goal in mind the discussion will become a rambling event which will end inconclusively. However, be prepared to change your objective if the meeting reveals new information, or if your team member proposes a course of action you had not considered, but would support.

Opening a counselling discussion is never easy. Your team member is likely to be experiencing mixed emotions. Therefore, tact is required. If you are too direct in your scene-setting then your team member is likely to go on to the defence from the start. The secret is to move into the questioning phase of your counselling as soon as possible.

Shown below are two examples of how NOT to open a counselling discussion:

> *Jim, I wanted to talk to you this morning about your poor timekeeping. You will have to do something about it.*
>
> *Bill, today's meeting is about the difficulties you have obviously been experiencing when compiling the production deadlines. Difficulties lead to mistakes and mistakes can cost the company a lot of money.*

Now regardless of whether Jim or Bill accepts that they are not meeting their obligations they will seek to defend themselves against criticism.

Compare the versions above with the following:

> *Jim, thanks for meeting me this morning, I want to get your views on your present role and on how you would like to see it develop.*
>
> *Bill, you have been responsible for preparing our production schedules for just over one month and today I would like to get your views on the issues you've encountered when handling this important task.*

In neither case was reference made to mistakes, faults or poor performance. In both cases the language is positive and encourages participation. There is no *"talk at"* approach. Instead the *"discuss with"* style is used.

Your first goal is to find out the reasons for the lack of punctuality and production difficulties. Until you understand the causes of the problems then you cannot work with your team member to find a solution.

Using your prepared structured questions you should aim to encourage your employee to reveal the difficulties he is experiencing. If you tell him there is a problem he may defend even the indefensible.

When asking your structured questions seek to use the PAST-PRESENT-FUTURE sequence i.e.:

— What has been done, experienced and achieved?

— What is being done, experienced and achieved?

— What will be done, experienced and achieved?

You need to remember that if you are counselling a person on a current difficulty then the causes of the problem lie in the past. These need to be identified before future action can be taken.

Remember to exclude the *"WHY"* prefix from your questions. However you express the word *"WHY"* it implies criticism. Substitute WHAT for WHY.

Take your time with the questioning phase of your counselling. Do not try to force your team member into acknowledging he or she has a *"problem"*.

As you pose your questions you need to be prepared for your team member raising concerns, resistances and objections.

Your team member could raise an objection or concern in the form of a question or statement, such as:

> *Are you saying I'm lazy?*
>
> *Don't you trust me?*
>
> *What are you leading up to?*
>
> *I do my job as well as I can, it's not easy.*

If the resistance comes in the form of an unstructured question, that is to say, one that aims to solicit a *"yes"* or *"no"* from you, do not respond with either. Instead steer the conversation away from the contentious issue into neutral territory. Here is an example of the steering technique. Your team member has asked you the question:

> *Are you saying I'm lazy?*

Your response could be:

> *Jim, my aim is to identify those factors that are preventing you from working to the deadlines and timings we both know are essential to our organisation.*

Once again your response is non-threatening and you have used the word *"WE"* to convey that the issue is a shared one.

If your team member raises a concern or objection in the form of a structured question, such as:

> *What are you leading up to?*

do not incorporate his or her wording in your response, for example:

> *I'm not leading up to anything.*

The repetition of the word reinforces the objection and sounds defensive.

Instead use a neutral reply, for example:

> *Bill, our discussion is about how I can help you to fulfil your new and increased responsibilities. Taking these on is a challenging task.*

The third category of objection arises most often when your team member acknowledges and accepts there is an issue to address, but he or she disagrees with your proposed solution or course of action.

When the objection/concern is raised your first task is to listen to the manner in which it is expressed. If the tone of voice is abrasive, direct, hostile or loud then there is little doubt that the objection is real and this needs to be handled using my Accept Agree Capitalise© approach. However, if the concern is expressed in a manner which is calm and dispassionate it could be that all your team member requires is reassurance that your ideas or suggestions will work. In this case use my Digging Techniques©.

What are Digging Techniques© and the AAC© approach to objection handling?

Digging Techniques are a means of identifying if the concern expressed by an individual is a real objection or an excuse, a stalling device or a masked request for re-assurance.

You use Digging Techniques© as follows:

1. Listen carefully to determine the nature of the concern.
2. Turn the concern back to your team member by using a question, for example:

   If we can resolve …

   If I could assure you …

   If I could demonstrate …

   If that were not an issue …

3. Conclude each question with the phrase – *"What then?"*

   You should pose your question in a relaxed and conversational manner otherwise your team member may react negatively. As you seek to master Digging Techniques the phrase *"What then?"* will help to prevent you from saying such things as:

   Would that be OK?

   Is that alright?

   Is there anything else worrying you?

These phrases can encourage your team member to raise new concerns.

Once you are comfortable using Digging Techniques you can eliminate the phrase *"What then?"* by simply raising your voice at the end of your question.

Once you have confirmed your team member's objection then you can use my AAC© technique.

AAC© stands for ACCEPT, AGREE and CAPITALISE. AAC© is based upon the psychology of doing the opposite of what the person you are counselling expects. Let me explain. When someone raises an objection he or she is inclined to expect you to respond in a defensive way with such phrases as:

> *Yes, but you have to appreciate …*

or

> *No, that's not the case …*

The *"yes, but"* response to employees objections is used all too often by managers. Have you ever analysed the phrase *"Yes, but"*. First of all it is a contradiction in terms. The respondent is actually saying *"Yes, no you are wrong"*. Secondly, it acts like a verbal head butt. Once used the recipient fights back from the blow.

This is how you use the AAC© technique:

ACCEPT — The objection or concern and thank your team member for raising the issue, for example:

> *John, thank you for making me aware of …*

or

> *Mary, I appreciate you raising the issue of …*

AGREE — Agree with the fact that you need to address the concern, for example:

> *I agree we need to address that …*

or

> *I agree we must certainly look at that …*

CAPITALISE — Here you turn the negative issue into a positive one by the use of such phrases as:

> *Your raising the subject of … gives me the opportunity to explain how we can address that.*

or

> *In fact, your raising your concern enables me to explain how …*

The first two parts of AAC© take the emotion out of the dialogue. After all how can your team member remain in a concerned or hostile state when you have accepted his right to raise his concern and agreed with the need to address it?

The capitalise stage of AAC© provides you with the opportunity to demonstrate the benefits to your team member of your idea/suggestions.

Here is an example of all three stages of AAC© being used. Your team member has expressed very strongly the objection of:

> *I haven't got the time to check everything, so mistakes are bound to occur.*

Your response:

> *John, thanks for raising the issue of the time you have available for your various tasks. I agree it is a challenge. In fact your raising the subject enables me to explain how we can reschedule a number of your jobs to give you the time you need to ensure the production schedules are always accurate.*

When counselling someone you can reduce the number of objections or concerns raised by taking two specific actions:

1. Invite your team member to propose his or her solution to the issue under discussion.
2. When you present your ideas ensure they are expressed in terms which are beneficial to your employee. It is all too easy to suggest a course of action in a manner that proclaims the advantages to you or your company and ignores those that apply to your employee.

Commit to paper all the counselling agreements you reach with your staff. I appreciate that counselling should be informal in nature. However, remember the old saying:

> *Verbal agreements aren't worth the paper they are written on*

Written agreements, even those that are short and succinct, help to prevent misunderstandings or misinterpretations.

Chapter 24

HOW CAN CORRECTIVE INTERVIEWS BE USED TO DEVELOP YOUR PEOPLE?

Many of us who have held management positions for a number of years know that our attempts to change peoples' behaviour through counselling are not always successful. On those occasions when an individual does not do and achieve what he or she said would be done and achieved, a CORRECTIVE INTERVIEW may be necessary.

The informality of a counselling discussion is replaced by a more formal meeting and the objective is to eliminate or, at least, minimise your team member's faults or failings, in such a way that he or she is strongly encouraged to remedy his or her shortcomings.

Whilst many corrective interviews take place when counselling has not produced the desired result, the nature and seriousness of your employee's shortcomings may necessitate you making a corrective interview your first activity. When you find yourself in a position where corrective action must be taken it is tempting to view the meeting as one which will resemble a mini-trial. Do not allow yourself to adopt the stance of prosecutor, judge and jury. A corrective interview should be viewed as a positive opportunity to bring about change.

How should you conduct a corrective interview? Here are thirteen guidelines to follow regardless of the nature of the corrective issue:

1. Make absolutely certain you have as many FACTS as possible. You cannot correct someone on the basis of rumour or conjecture.
2. Arrange to meet your team member in a setting where you can ensure privacy and freedom from interruptions.
3. As with a counselling discussion seek to conduct a corrective interview early in the day and at the beginning of the week.
4. Do not enter into a corrective interview with a set course of action in mind. By this statement I do not mean that you should not consider appropriate courses of action. However, you need to remain prepared to hear your employee's point of view.
5. Open the discussion on a friendly note and avoid showing signs of annoyance, prejudice, pre-conceived ideas or personal animosity.

I appreciate that you may be feeling disappointed that your team member has let you and the company down. However, if a negative attitude is apparent on your face then the discussion is likely to start at a low point and go down even further.

6. Set the scene for your discussions by describing in concise and unemotive terms why you have called the meeting. Think carefully about your choice of words.

   Shown below is an example of how not to set the scene:

   > *Jim, I was horrified yesterday to receive a call from David Ryan at Avalon Manufacturing in which he said that the attitude you demonstrated throughout your last appointment with him was nothing short of arrogant. He's our biggest customer. We can't afford to lose his account and I want to discuss what you are going to do to placate him.*

   Jim has been found guilty and he didn't even have the benefit of a trial!

   Clearly something has gone wrong. But the manager has only received David Ryan's version of the events which are alleged to have taken place. The facts of the matter (and the truth) may be somewhat different.

   Here is another example of scene-setting. In this instance a production employee was counselled four weeks ago on his poor timekeeping and during the last month the employee has been late on four occasions:

   > *Steve, you will recall that four weeks ago we discussed the subject of your timekeeping and at the end of the meeting we agreed upon a series of actions that would enable you to be on-site each morning at least five minutes before your scheduled start time. Today I would like to review how you have acted upon those agreements and what has resulted.*

   The style of the opening contrasts dramatically with that used by Jim's manager. No charged words such as *"horrified"* were used. No indication was given of the production manager's attitude towards the employee's late arrivals – in fact they were not mentioned and the opening concluded with the manager inviting the employee to discuss what has resulted from the previous agreements.

7. Progress the discussion by inviting your team member to give his assessment of the situation. For the example shown above you could say:

> *So Steve, how successful do you consider you have been in the last month at getting here on time every day?*

8. Proceed with your questioning to identify what are the causes of the problem. Invite your team member to assess the situation. At this stage the employee may offer extenuating circumstances for his or her late arrivals.
9. Summarise what you both see as the causes of the problem.
10. Invite your team member to prescribe the corrective action. Ask him to prepare an ACTION PLAN.
11. Review the proposed contents of the Action Plan and reach agreements.
12. Conclude the discussions on a positive note by reinforcing your commitment to help your team member.
13. Confirm the date, time and location of your next review meeting regarding the matter in question.

The approach I have recommended calls for you to show patience and to place the onus on your team member. If you are tempted to say to yourself:

> *But why can't I just get to the point quickly by telling the employee what's wrong?*

Remember the saying:

> *Statements create confrontation, questions stimulate communication*

Your corrective interviews should be designed and conducted in order to bring an employee back on track. Whilst you are addressing a negative issue corrective interviews can provide you with the opportunity to re-focus and motivate employees.

Chapter 25

DO YOU USE *"JOB ROTATION"* AS A MEANS TO DEVELOP YOUR STAFF?

Job rotation, even if only for a short period, is one of the most effective means of helping staff to realise their potential and to identify what they are most suited to do within your company. However, like all personnel development activities it must be planned in detail. You need to consider a variety of factors, including:

— Which jobs within my department and the company as a whole provide ideal vehicles for developing employees?

— What do I want to achieve from a planned programme of rotation? (Identify/define your objectives)

— Who has the right aptitude for a temporary job move?

— What will the employee(s) gain from job rotation?

— For how long should each person fulfil the temporary role?

— How can I win other directors or managers support for a job rotation programme?

— How can I prepare individuals for their moves?

— What difficulties could arise from job rotation?

— How can these be prevented?

Your starting point for job rotation is to look at the people and roles within your own department, section or function and address each of the questions shown above. Then raise the issue of job rotation with your fellow directors and managers in order to identify if a co-ordinated, company-wide programme can be initiated. Job rotation should always be linked to the subject of EMPLOYEE SUCCESSION PLANNING.

Regrettably far too many companies pay lip service to the issue of succession planning. They express their recognition of the importance of identifying the supervisors, managers and directors of tomorrow – but then do little to identify and develop these people.

To check whether you are committed to employee succession planning answer the following questions:

> *How many employees of your company are due to retire within the next five years?*
>
> *In which departments?*
>
> *In which job functions?*
>
> *At what levels?*
>
> *How many employees do you expect to seek early retirement?*
>
> *From which departments?*
>
> *From which job functions?*
>
> *At what levels?*
>
> *How many employees do you anticipate will leave the company of their own volition in the next five years?* (Review your staff turnover records for the last two years to identify a possible pattern.)
>
> *How many employees do you expect to dismiss from your company in the next five years?* (Review your dismissal record for the last two years to identify if there is a pattern.)
>
> *How many people have died whilst in your employment in the last five years?*
>
> *Of what causes?*
>
> *From which departments?*
>
> *At what levels?*

If you have difficulty answering any of these questions you may be sitting on a time bomb of your own making.

Job rotation offers you the opportunity to achieve multi-skilling within your organisation and it can help to reduce boredom and staff turnover among employees.

CHAPTER 26

PERFORMANCE REVIEWS – OPPORTUNITIES TO ENCOURAGE YOUR STAFF TO DEVELOP

It is a rare employee that does not want to know what his or her boss thinks of his or her performance. However, the manner in which that feedback is given can have a huge impact on an employee's morale, motivation and, therefore, desire to enhance his or her performance.

This chapter discusses the following issues:

— What constitutes a *"Performance Review"?*

— The benefits Performance Reviews can bring

— How to formalise Performance Reviews

— How to conduct Performance Reviews

WHAT IS MEANT BY THE TERM *"PERFORMANCE REVIEW"*?

It is a formal discussion between a manager and an employee on the latter's performance over a prescribed period of time. It involves a mutual exchange of views and opinions on a team member's strengths and shortcomings and it should result in an agreed course of action for both the manager and employee. When conducted effectively performance reviews can achieve a number of important results, including:

— improved morale and individual motivation

— better two-way communication between a manager and a team member

— individual recognition of personal strengths and weaknesses and appropriate corrective action

— more management involvement in the human relationship aspects of the job

— improved job performance

— more individual job satisfaction and, in the long term, promotion

However, what is critical, is whether they are conducted effectively. The starting point for achieving this goal is the design of the performance review document.

In theory, a performance review can be undertaken without a note being taken. However, there are many benefits to be gained from the production of a formal performance review document.

When a manager reviews an employee's performance his or her starting point tends to be the MEASURABLE RESULTS that person has achieved over a given period. For example salesman can be measured on number of orders secured, income generated, profit secured etc. Production staff can be assessed by the number of units they produce. Whilst numerical measurements can be important, they do not provide a manager with a complete picture of an individual's performance.

Numerical measurements of performance let the manager know WHAT an employee has achieved. However, they do not enable the manager to determine HOW WELL the employee has performed.

Numerical measurements can sometimes be misleading. For example, a salesman may achieve *"110% of his budget"*. But did he succeed in spite of his efforts, because he had a unique product or a territory with huge business potential? Another salesman may achieve *"86% of his budget"*. But his products may have been surpassed by those of other manufacturers or his products may be priced too highly.

Astute managers consider numerical measurements in conjunction with their assessment of HOW WELL an individual fulfils his or her job. An individual's effectiveness (how well the job is performed) is determined by his or her ATTITUDES, KNOWLEDGE and SKILLS and is influenced by the individual's PERSONALITY.

In order to assess how well one of your staff performs you need to start by drawing up a list of the Attitudes, Knowledge and Skills you expect the job holder to possess and to demonstrate.

When undertaking this task bear the following points in mind:

1. An ATTITUDE is an individual's frame of mind or disposition. Under this heading examples can include:

   — Enthusiastic — Self-Motivated
   — Determined — Dedicated

   As you consider each heading beware of duplication, for example, *"self-motivated"* and *"self-starter"* or *"committed"* and *"determined"*.

   Ensure you can define clearly the term you select. If you are not clear in your definition how are you going to assess your team member's quality?

2. KNOWLEDGE is the information an individual has gained through study, experience and the fulfilment of various jobs.

3. A SKILL is the application of acquired knowledge.

Although you will use your AKS Profile as the basis for your review of your team member's performance you will also find that it will serve another valuable purpose. Your list represents the qualities you would look for in a new employee. Therefore, when you embark upon a recruitment campaign you can use the list as a reference document.

Attitudes have the most important influence on an employee's performance – because they are the qualities which are influenced most easily and frequently by events. As a consequence when you conduct initial interviews with prospective employees you should focus the majority of your efforts on the identification of the applicant's attitudes. Once again you use the power of structured questioning. Applicants can and often do profess to having particular knowledge and skills. However, such claims need to be VERIFIED and TESTED.

Claimed knowledge can be verified through such items as exam results, the nature of qualifications secured, and certificates. Skills need to be tested in practical ways, for each skill within your AKS Profile you need to develop a test that will confirm or otherwise an individual's level of competence.

AKS Profiles vary in size in relation to the seniority and complexity of a job. For example an AKS Profile for a main board Director in a large Plc Company could comprise at least sixty headings. Whereas an AKS Profile for a junior production worker might contain between fifteen and twenty headings.

Your AKS Profile for each of the job functions within your team provides you with the basis for assessing how well each person has fulfilled his or her role over a prescribed period. But your review will be more meaningful if you apply a QUANTIFIABLE assessment to each of the qualitative aspects of an individual's performance.

Let me introduce you to my FORCED CHOICE RATING SYSTEM.

The system involves you in assessing each attitude, knowledge and skill heading by means of a NUMERICAL RATING – that of 2, 4, 6 or 8.

The "4" rating represents the minimum standard of performance you expect the individual to achieve.

The forced choice rating does not allow you to choose the soft option of an average rating. Your team member either achieves your minimum standard of performance (4) or is above or below it.

To differentiate between each rating it is desirable to produce a WORD PICTURE for each of the 2, 4, 6, 8 marks. For example, if you incorporated LISTENING within your skills list then the 2-4-6-8 ratings could be described as follows:

2 = Rarely listens to understand the issues raised by colleagues and customers.

4 = Endeavours to listen in order to understand his contacts remarks but is not consistent in his behaviour.

6 = On most occasions seeks to listen to rather than just hear what people say.

8 = Consistently demonstrates his ability to listen, interpret and understand points made to him by customers and colleagues.

If you have 40 headings within your AKS Profile then the production of 160 word pictures is a challenging and even daunting task. Therefore, I recommend to many managers the following:

— Always produce a word picture for the "4" rating for each of your headings within an AKS Profile.

— Issue these word pictures with the performance review document to your team member.

— Use the "4" rating as a basis for discussion with your team member in order to determine if he or she considers he or she warrants a 2-4-6 or 8 rating.

When you issue your team members with the performance review document advise them that you want them to conduct a self-assessment in order to determine their own ratings. These ratings can then be discussed with you. Self-assessment often results in an individual being more critical of his or her performance than you would be. In turn that situation provides you with an opportunity to motivate the individual by advising him or her that he or she has been over-critical.

The frequency of performance reviews is often a subject for some debate. Many organisations have, what they refer to as, *"annual appraisals"*. If you only sit down and review your team members performance once a year then what good does this serve? Can you remember accurately how well the person performed eleven months ago? How can you arrive at a rating that embraces a twelve-month period during which the team member's performance could have changed dramatically? If you conduct an annual review and are critical of how well someone performed during the first quarter aren't you encouraging that person to say……. *"If I was performing badly then why did you wait nine months to tell me?"* For most job roles I recommend a QUARTERLY REVIEW.

With your AKS Profile and word pictures prepared how do you conduct a performance review discussion? Here are some guidelines:

1. A performance review enables you to evaluate (with your team member) how well she or he performs his or her job. You are examining the qualitative aspects of the individual's performance and, although you use the

Forced Choice Numerical Rating System (2-4-6-8) to quantify the review, it is impossible to eliminate subjectivity from the discussion. You can reduce the subjective element by ensuring that your evaluations are based on your OBSERVATIONS of individuals fulfilling their job and EVIDENCE of the results of their efforts.

2. If you have not been able to observe your team member demonstrating a particular attitude, knowledge or skill during the period of the review you cannot award a performance rating. In this event you should enter the letters NEA (No Evidence Available) in the appropriate review column. The inclusion of NEA should focus your mind on why you have not seen your team member fulfil that particular aspect of his or her job. Have you spent insufficient time with the individual? Have you failed to organise your activities in order to see him or her demonstrate the particular attitudes, knowledge or skills?

   The inclusion of two or three NEA insertions means that your overall Minimum Standard of Performance drops, for example:

Number of AKS Headings	:	30
MSOP	:	120
Number of NEA Insertions	:	3
Reduced MSOP	:	108

3. Always ensure your evaluation covers the complete review period. You must avoid focusing on the most recent and easily remembered events and results.

4. Throughout the review encourage your team member to identify the actions he or she needs to take to capitalise still further on his or her strengths and to eliminate (or at least reduce the effects of) shortcomings.

5. Base your communication style on my **ACE©** approach. **ACE** stands for:

   Analyse performance

   Counsel

   Encourage action

6. Do not enter into a performance review in a fixed frame of mind. You will have your views on an individual's performance – but that person has his or her views. He or she should be encouraged to express these openly and you need to be prepared to change your mind and eliminate prejudices.

7. A performance review will identify or confirm an individual's shortcomings. These revelations or confirmations necessitate you DEMONSTRATING HOW shortcomings can be eliminated. You should never state what you want someone to do or change unless you can show that person how

to make the change or undertake the new action.

8. As action areas are identified during the performance review ensure these are not restricted to those which your team member should undertake. Be seen to accept your own action commitments.
9. Be prepared to take TIME over each performance review. If your team member considers the review is being rushed then he or she may believe that you are *"just going through the motions"*, rather than demonstrating a genuine interest in his or her performance and how it can be developed.
10. Ensure the performance review is a two-way process.
11. Remember that performance reviews are not about giving criticism, they are about achieving improvements.
12. Do not focus exclusively on negative issues and beware of using the wrong vocabulary e.g. "What do you think you have done *badly* this quarter?".
13. Record action agreements within an Action Plan.
14. Always aim to end a performance review on a high note. I appreciate that a review cannot always be a "good news" event. On the other hand if your team member leaves the review thinking he or she has experienced a corrective interview rather than a motivational discussion, the event has failed.

Performance reviews should play a critical part in the development of your staff since they enable you to measure not only improvements in your team members' performance but also your own effectiveness as a developer of people.

Refer to Checklist nine on page 176 when you are preparing performance reviews.

CHAPTER 27

CUSTOMER CARE – IT'S EVERYONE'S AFFAIR

Whenever I meet managing directors with whom I have not worked in the past I seek an opportunity to ask the following question:

What are you in business to achieve?

All too often the immediate response is either:

To make money

or

To make profits

I always encourage managing directors to reflect a little longer on the question and to reconsider their response.

On some occasions managing directors stick to their original reply. Others add such items as:

Producing a satisfactory return for shareholders

or

Providing employment opportunities

Regrettably I cannot recall one occasion on which the managing director gave me the reply I sought. That of:

To satisfy customers consistently

You see it is all a question of focus. If directors are preoccupied with "making profit" then they are often overly cost-conscious. They constantly look for ways to avoid spending money.

Now I am as concerned as every managing director about ensuring that expenditure is always justifiable. However, with my focus on SATISFYING CUSTOMERS CONSISTENTLY I know that if I achieve that goal then my company will make lots of profit.

Satisfying customers consistently does not just happen. It has to be planned, organised and monitored carefully.

If directors and managers wish to develop their company then they have to develop the CUSTOMER CARE SKILLS of each employee.

Over the last twenty years developments in technological aids have contributed to a situation where the differences between the products and services provided by industry and commerce have reduced substantially. As a consequence, the development of employee skills represents the most significant area of opportunity for giving companies that "competitive edge".

Skill development is not restricted to those items which are exclusively job-related, e.g. accountancy, research or technical. The area of skill development that transcends departmental/job function boundaries is that of client/customer relations – or as it has become known, CUSTOMER CARE.

CUSTOMER CARE can be defined as:

> *Identifying and satisfying the primary needs and wants of customers, on a consistent basis and, in a manner which ensures these customers* <u>*want*</u> *to maintain their business relationship with your organisation.*

The practice of customer care is not a new concept. However, over the last ten years it has gained prominence and recognition in its own right. Customer care will continue to grow in importance as service industries grow in size and number. This is inevitable as technology reduces the need for labour to produce goods.

Customer care doesn't always require a company to incur costs. Tact, politeness and a smile cost nothing.

But some major organisations have spent millions of pounds on customer care programmes. The motives behind the investments have been sound – but has there been a healthy return on such investments? I pose the question not to obtain an answer but to introduce you to ideas that will help you to develop the customer care skills of your staff in ways that produce a satisfying return.

At this point it is worth considering the question:

> *What is a CUSTOMER?*

The answer to this question may appear to be simple: But is it?

WHAT IS A CUSTOMER?

A customer is anyone who:

- has purchased from you in the past
- could purchase from you in the future
- could influence other peoples' attitudes towards your company.

A customer is not dependent on us ...... we are dependent on him or her.

A customer is not an interruption to our work – he or she is the purpose of it.

A customer is not someone with whom to argue or match wits. Nobody ever won an argument with a customer.

A customer is a person who brings us his or her wants. It is our job to handle those wants profitably for the customer as well as for ourselves.

WHAT DOES OUR CUSTOMER WANT FROM US?

Most employees would answer this question with the response:

The specific service or product we provide.

Oh, that it were that simple.

Customers want far more than the basic product or service.

Each of your existing or potential customers has his or her own W.I.N.E© list.

My acronym for W.I.N.E stands for:

Wants
Interests
Needs
and Expectations

WANTS are an individual's desires. They are emotionally based, often irrational and sometimes difficult to define – but they are nonetheless very real.

INTERESTS are an individual's personal concerns or pre-occupations. We all have personal interests which motivate us to make specific decisions.

NEEDS are peoples' essential requirements. They are predominately logical in nature, often easy to define and to quantify.

EXPECTATIONS are the views people have formed primarily through past experiences.

You can never assume or guess your customers W.I.N.E list. You and your team members must seek to identify, define, quantify and prioritise your customers requirements on an ongoing basis. Maintaining this awareness calls for employees to develop their observation, listening and questioning skills.

WHAT TURNS YOUR CUSTOMER OFF?

Customers' attitudes towards you and your company are conditioned by physical and mental experiences. PHYSICAL experiences are derived from the use of your products and services. MENTAL experiences are the feelings stimulated by the customers' contact with you and other members of your staff.

Successful customer care is based upon employees combining the RIGHT PERSONAL ATTITUDES and ATTRIBUTES with COMPANY and PRODUCT KNOWLEDGE and COMMUNICATION SKILLS.

Customers are turned off primarily by:

— Poor product quality

— Poor service

— Poor sense of value

BUT particularly by:

— Poor response to me, that is making me as a customer feel I am unimportant and being treated accordingly.

Disgruntled customers talk to your prospective customers and disgruntled customers advertise your inefficiency.

What are some of the practical initiatives and actions you can take to demonstrate to your customers your desire, and that of your staff, to provide real "customer care"?

1. CUSTOMER CARE doesn't just happen – there has to be EDUCATION.

   The education of employees should begin during their induction programme. Does the induction programme for each new employee within your company include a "customer care" component? Is that component seen to be as important as (and ideally more important than) such mechanical issues as "company policies and procedures", "administration", "product knowledge"?

   Many companies should reflect upon Disney World's approach to inducting its road sweepers and rubbish collectors. Each new litter collector receives a five day induction course. Ten minutes is spent teaching them how to sweep the roads and collect litter. The remaining time is devoted to educating them in how to relate to Disney World's guests.

   During each employee's induction programme give specific attention to the company's:

   — commitment to

   — approach towards

   — minimum standards for

   CUSTOMER CARE

In addition, the training must involve ROLE-PLAY work, in which real customer situations are used – from the sales enquiry stage to that of customer conflict.

Ongoing development is then required to ensure staff are CONSISTENT in the positive management of customers. Consider conducting an annual audit of customer care practices as a way of evaluating if your education and training is working.

2. MINIMUM STANDARDS OF PERFORMANCE for job related tasks.

   In an effective customer care orientated company, employees believe in the saying "right first time". As a consequence, they understand the need for, and benefits to be derived from, the attainment (and ideally surpassment) of minimum standards of performance.

   For those customer care activities that constitute part of an employee's job, it should always be possible for you to identify such minimum performance standards.

   Examples could include:

   — speed of telephone response (the three ring rule)

   — telephone manner

   — speed of service

   — accuracy of service

   — legibility of correspondence

   — the incidence of grammatical or spelling errors

   — pro-active (rather than reactive) behaviour

3. Provide INCENTIVES to encourage employees to demonstrate and sustain their interest in CUSTOMER CARE.

   Customer care and staff care go hand in hand. Never forget that whenever you improve an aspect of customer service, then you should consider whether equal attention is being given to employee care. For example, if you improve the facade of your buildings – you should not ignore the condition of the staff toilets!

   Customer care relies on employees' motivation. Although, as I have pointed out already in this book, motivation is a complex issue, you should give particular attention to the issues of FINANCIAL REWARDS, RECOGNITION and OPPORTUNITY.

Financial reward could come through modified salary levels, commission or bonuses. Recognition can be given in the form of awards or public acclaim. Opportunity could take the form of job promotion or increased responsibility.

4. Customer care necessitates POSITIVE COMMUNICATION.

   One of the most common misunderstandings associated with caring for the customer, is that an employee needs to be either subservient, servile or ingratiating. No one would admit openly to being any of these things, but regrettably, such characteristics are displayed, when employees approach customers in a less than positive manner.

   Educate and encourage your staff to communicate positively with customers on ALL occasions.

   Shown below are some typical examples of how negative communication can be turned into positive dialogue.

NEGATIVE	POSITIVE
Do you need any help?	*How can I help?*
It's not my department	*I don't know the answer but I'll find out for you. When would you like me to call you?*
Is there a problem?	*How can I help?*

   Employees who communicate positively are individuals who accept ownership of an issue. The term ownership means seeing an issue through to its conclusion.

5. PRACTICE what you PREACH.

   You cannot propound the importance of customer care, unless you employ such principles all the time. Managers must avoid a situation where staff describe them as individuals who adopt the practice of:

   Don't do as I do – just do as I say

   When staff are asked to commit themselves to customer care, then managers are asking them to become more actively involved in all aspects of the business. You must practice the same principle and get out from behind your desk.

   Involvement isn't just desirable – it's essential.

6. Treat COMPLAINTS AS OPPORTUNITIES and not problems.

   Perhaps the statement shown above may come as something of a surprise, but it highlights the attitude every one of us should have towards dealing with complaints.

Even in the most efficient companies, things can and do go wrong and customers will complain. However, if our reaction is always defensive, then we may well win the battle but lose the war.

Turning a complaining customer into a loyal customer is a skilled business and requires you and your team members to:

- LISTEN ATTENTIVELY. You may be the first person to hear the story. Let them get it out of their system. An empathetic ear can defuse the most explosive situation.
- ACKNOWLEDGE THE CUSTOMER'S VIEWPOINT. Most people have perfectly good reasons for complaining and even if you think they do not, it does no harm to try and see things from their point of view.
- APOLOGISE. Do not grovel. Be polite – but don't overdo it!
- FIND A SOLUTION. Move quickly from the nature and effects of the complaint to what you can do to help. Do not dwell on the problem, it only aggravates. Question the customer to find out the most acceptable timescales and expectations.
- REACH A CONCLUSION. Provide a solution or explain what action will be taken, or, take the customer to the person who CAN solve the problem. Do not make promises that someone else cannot keep.
- FOLLOW THROUGH. Check subsequently on the progress of any action or contact with the customer, to make sure that he is happy.
- BE SINCERE. Treat your customer as you would like to be treated yourself. We all know the sheer frustration of an ignored complaint.
- ANTICIPATE complaints before they occur. Customers who expect a delivery on Monday morning are more impressed with your company, if you phone to explain any delay rather than leave the customer to telephone to register his annoyance. If the customers know you are trying, they will be more sympathetic if things go wrong.

But what about "difficult" customers – the ones who cause scenes, make personal remarks, stand aloof, or look with the deepest suspicion on ourselves and the organisation we represent? There are tried and tested ways of dealing with such "problem" customers:

- ANGER. Never argue – it gets you nowhere but into deeper trouble. Establish the reason for the anger, apologise, investigate the matter and deal with it immediately.
- RUDENESS. Never return the rudeness – do not get involved and do not take any remarks personally – they are caused by anger with your

organisation. It is your job to dissipate that anger and you cannot do that by taking offence. If possible, remove the loud, aggressive person to an office or another room. This has the result of getting him away from "his territory" on to your home ground and also taking him away from an audience.

- SUSPICION. Make sure you have an impeccable knowledge of your service and goods. Be as direct and open as possible. Do not walk into the trap of talking yourself into trouble – take your time and let the customer do most of the talking.
- SILENCE. Use structured questioning to gather information about what might be wrong. If the customer does not seem to want to communicate, allow him or her time, draw him/her out, but do not be too talkative.

  During the 1960s and 1970s, it was common to find a "complaints department" in major organisations. Very often, such departments were staffed by people who saw their role as "the company's first line of defence". Thankfully, attitudes have changed, but just take a look at your own organisation.

  Do you have a customer service or customer satisfaction team? Do your staff and colleagues approach complaints in a defensive or in a pro-active manner?

  When you, or your colleagues, encounter a customer who is less than happy with your organisation, does that "moment of truth" (as Jan Caslow, Managing Director of Scandinavian Airways described it) result in a positive, or negative, outcome for your company?

  That "Moment of Truth" is every contact with a customer.

7. Promote CUSTOMER CARE over the telephone.

   How often has your attitude towards a company been affected negatively, by the way in which you have been greeted during your telephone call to that organisation? Perhaps you have been subjected to one or more of the following responses:

   — The "let's keep them hanging on in silence"

   — The "let's play them our recorded musical tape at least fifteen times"

   — The "let's not answer until it rings at least ten times"

   — The "let's tell them how busy we are, by expressing that immortal phrase – I've got another six people waiting"

   — The "let's plead ignorance by saying – I'm new here"

— The "let's cut you off and blame it on the phone company"

— The "you must have got the wrong number"

— The "no, I don't recall you phoning last week"

— The "no, he's left and I don't know who is dealing with it now"

Amusing? – Only if you *haven't* experienced these frustrations.

Develop each member of your team to answer calls promptly, to smile as they greet customers and to thank callers.

To encourage your team members to deliver consistently high levels of customer care introduce them to my acronym:

Communication	The initiative must be yours
Understanding	Always try to see the customer's point of view
Sincerity	If you are not sincere it will show through
Tolerance	It is essential and not merely desirable
Opportunism	Look for opportunities to build on customer relationships
Motivation	Encourage others to share your motivation for customer care
Enthusiasm	It is infectious and stimulates business relationships
Resilience	Bounce back from the inevitable knocks encountered in business
Creativity	Always look for new ways to improve the organisation, service and results
Appearance	First impressions are important
Responsiveness	The speed of your response reflects the importance you attach to your customer
Effectiveness	Do the right job as well as doing the job right

and the old Scottish proverb …

> *Looking after your customer is not merely good manners – it's good business too.*

Chapter 28

DEVELOP YOUR PEOPLE TO MANAGE CHANGE

It has often been said that:

The only thing that is constant in life is change

But what do we mean by the word “change”? In dictionary terms, it means to “alter” or “vary”. But the word has a unique ability to conjure up an immense variety of pictures within our minds, pictures which have both pleasing and distasteful associations.

As you seek to develop your company today you are faced with changes that are occurring faster, are less predictable and more impactful and more varied in their nature than ever before. As a consequence many of your team members may be resistant to change. After all few people would admit to liking change.

Negative reactions to change are predominately emotional in nature. I am sure you can recall occasions on which your staff reacted emotionally to a proposed change, which, when considered logically, made a great deal of sense. Emotions so often overrule common sense. Employees reactions to change can be stimulated by a multitude of factors including:

— age

— satisfaction

— intellect

— risk

— health

— potential consequences

— effort

— anticipated results

However, at the root of so many reactions to change is FEAR.

What can you do to offset your team members fear of change and to develop their desire to see change as an ally and not an adversary?

Your aim must be to lead by example and here are six actions you can take:

1. Show each of your team members that you have an "open-minded" approach to change. Always be prepared to listen and evaluate proposed changes, rather than dismiss ideas and suggestions out of hand.

2. Demonstrate a flexibility in your thinking.

   Be prepared to modify your attitudes and concede that some of your past ideas and views have been based upon prejudice rather than rational thought.

3. Be prepared for frustrations and disappointments.

   Changes do not always result in instant success or improvements. Look upon disappointments as learning opportunities and not as events which stimulate you to express criticism. Remind your staff of the words of the opera singer, Beverley Sills "You may be disappointed if you fail, but you are doomed if you don't try."

4. Be prepared to reappraise your working methods and effectiveness.

   Although we can all benefit from feedback from others on our performance we must ultimately become our most critical assessor.

   By assessing your strengths and shortcomings you can establish the base line against which changes should be made.

5. Remove all traces of indifference you may have had in the past, over the need to change.

   In the future, no one will be able to say... "I will not be affected".

6. Demonstrate a desire to acquire new skills.

   Business people today cannot rely solely on their "experience" because experience is concerned with what has happened and not necessarily with what will happen.

For your company to develop your people must embrace change. They will only be responsive to change when you are seen to be the architect, implementer and supporter of change. Show them that FEAR is just False Expectations Appearing to be Real.

Chapter 29

HOW CAN YOU STIMULATE THE CREATIVITY OF YOUR TEAM MEMBERS?

Successful companies engender an atmosphere of creativity. They encourage individuals to challenge the norm and to express new ideas.

How can this be done?

Consider the following methods:

1. Ask all members of your team to try to improve ONE specific aspect of their work each week or month.

   Individuals need to focus upon the aspects of their job which are within their control.

   When you introduce this idea some of your staff may feel that they cannot be too radical in their thinking or recommendations. Encourage them to be as radical as they like. However, at the same time ask them to present their ideas accompanied by a list of the POSITIVE RESULTS they consider would be achieved from making their recommended changes.

   Incidentally, many of the employees I have met and worked with over the years appear to be easily influenced by TINA. TINA is my acronym for There Is No Alternative. When you have undertaken a job, or a series of tasks, in a particular way for a long time you can be inclined to convince yourself that what you do is the best way and There Is No Alternative. TINA stems from individuals' reluctance to change and from the inclination within many of us to accept the status quo. Let your staff know that TINA is a very unwelcome visitor to your company!

2. Create an IDEAS BOARD.

   This is a board on which employees write or post their ideas. The board should be placed in a central or easily accessible location. You can stimulate specific ideas by placing a QUESTION in the centre of the board. For example:

   > *HOW CAN WE INCREASE OUR CUSTOMER RETENTION FIGURES?*

or

WHAT ACTIONS DO WE NEED TO TAKE TO BECOME NO.1 IN OUR MARKET?

or

HOW CAN WE CAPITALISE STILL FURTHER ON THE STRENGTHS OF OUR COMPANY?

or

HOW CAN WE ATTRACT NEW CUSTOMERS TO OUR COMPANY?

Your questions need to be specific in nature but not restrictive. In addition, they should always be ACTION-ORIENTATED. The use of the HOW prefix to a question helps to ensure this is achieved.

3. Introduce a QUARTERLY "IDEAS LOTTERY".

   The lottery works as follows. Each time an employee submits a creative idea to you he or she receives one half of a numbered ticket. The other half goes into a lottery ideas box. At the end of the quarter one ticket is picked (at random) from the lottery draw box and you award a prize to the person whose number is chosen.

   There should be no restriction on the number of tickets awarded to submitters of ideas. You want to encourage ideas and individuals will recognise that their chances of winning a prize are increased in relation to their creativity.

   Do not put restrictions on the types of creative idea individuals should submit. The LOTTERY DRAW has another advantage for employees. The prize is awarded solely on the number of the ticket drawn. No assessment or evaluation is made of each idea submitted.

4. Provide a CREATIVE CORNER within your offices, building or factory.

   The Creative Corner is a room where people are encouraged to go to think, to solve problems and to consider new ideas.

   The Creative Corner should be a light, airy and colourful room. It should have comfortable seating, as well as some desk space for people who wish to use computers. It can contain books, videos and games on creativity.

As you read my recommendation for a Creative Corner you may be wondering if employees would simply retreat to the room in order to escape from work. Perhaps you are thinking that the room will become a place in which people will just chat, read newspapers or complete crosswords. In those companies in which I have promoted the Creative Corner concept I have found that the majority of employees do not abuse the facility. They welcome the opportunity to THINK, to muse, to reflect and to open their minds to new ideas. If you fail to engender a desire amongst your team to think and to be creative then you will be surrounded by individuals who work only to procedures and instruction. As a consequence your company will not develop.

5. Establish INNOVATION GROUPS within your company.

   Innovation Groups comprise four or five employees drawn from different job functions but who share a similar status. The group meets once a month (or every six weeks) during a lunchtime to brainstorm and discuss new ideas.

   The group does not discuss how they can change things within the company or within a specific department. Their focus is solely on the creation of something NEW. Their aim is to seek INNOVATION and not imitation.

   Innovation groups should appoint their own chairperson and that individual should be different each time the group meets. I always recommend that innovation groups meet for no more than forty-five minutes. This restricted time focuses the members' minds. Many of the companies in which I have introduced innovation groups acknowledge that individuals are devoting their lunchtime to the meeting and as a form of thanks these companies provide a buffet lunch for the group.

   I also recommend that innovation groups meet on no more than four occasions before the composition of the group is changed. If the same people meet on more than three/four occasions the freshness of their thinking reduces and the results of their discussions are often disappointing.

6. Establish a *"CREATIVE EMPLOYEE CORRIDOR OF FAME"*.

   Your objective is to select a corridor within your building which is a busy traffic route for employees and visitors and within this corridor install photographs of those employees who have created outstanding ideas for the company. The photographs should be accompanied by the name of the employee and details of his or her idea and the benefits it has brought to the company.

7. Set *"CREATIVITY GOALS"*.

   Creativity Goals are new ideas targets set each for each employee on a monthly or quarterly basis.

   You may consider giving an employee a target for ideas generation to be strange. However, many successful authors and inventors have found that by forcing themselves to generate ideas, the ideas come. For example, Thomas Edison used this method. He targeted himself to create one minor invention every ten days and a major invention every six months.

8. Change employees RESPONSES in meetings.

   All too often when ideas are expressed during business meetings attendees can be heard to say, "Yes, but ... ". This response becomes a mindset and it stimulates negativity amongst the whole group. Individuals focus on what is wrong with an idea and not upon its merits.

   To change peoples' attitudes and responses insist that when a colleague puts forward an idea the response of "Yes, and ... " and not *"yes, but ..."* follows. The *"yes and ... "* response builds upon the idea and encourages people to consider how the idea can be developed and implemented.

9. Invite employees from different departments to brainstorming/problem-solving sessions. Invite them to solve your problem. Their objectivity and lack of intimate knowledge of a problem can provide the key to a solution. All too often we are so close to our own problems that we cannot, or will not, see the solutions available to us.

10. Most employees have a tendency to use one side of their brain in preference to the other. Left-brained staff are rational thinkers and right-brained employees are intuitive thinkers. To create a new approach to their thinking ask your left-brained staff to come up with creative, intuitive, irrational and unconventional ideas. Then ask your right-brained staff to come up with new logical, rational and practical ideas.

There have been many debates on whether people are born with creative powers or whether these powers can be learned. I am not going to join the debate. Instead I will reflect upon my own experience of developing people over the last twenty-five years. I have found that if you encourage people to think the unthinkable and pursue the impossible then creativity flourishes.

Refer to Appendix six and Checklist ten on page 157 and page 177.

Chapter 30

ARE YOU SELLING YOUR STAFF THE BENEFITS OF *"SELF-DEVELOPMENT"*?

Although you should be the main on-going source of training for your team members it is important to encourage each person to take responsibility for his or her own development. Individuals who express a desire to advance within their careers need to be advised on what activities they should undertake that will be relevant to their goals. They also need advice on what types of training to avoid. Giving such advice obligates you to gain a thorough understanding of the nature and extent of the training and development that can be obtained from the open market place.

Chapter 31

IN SUMMARY

Training and developing people has a great deal in common with the activities undertaken within the construction industry. It is always easier to knock something down than to construct a durable and appreciated building. Knocking people down can be done with just one ill-conceived remark. Building individuals' confidence and competence takes time, considerable effort and genuine care. However, the rewards can be immense for you and your company.

Good luck, *"Developing People to Develop your Company"*.

APPENDICES

Appendix 1

PERSONAL ACTION PLAN

Page …. of.

YOUR NAME:		**DATE:**	
WHAT IS TO BE DONE	**HOW IT IS TO BE DONE**	**BY WHEN**	**IN ORDER TO ACHIEVE THIS RESULT**

Model Document

Appendix 2

GROUP ACTION PLAN

Page .... of.

GROUP MEMBERS NAMES:		**DATE:**	
WHAT IS TO BE DONE	**HOW IT IS TO BE DONE**	**BY WHEN**	**IN ORDER TO ACHIEVE THIS RESULT**

Model Document

APPENDIX 3

TRAINING AND DEVELOPMENT PLAN (Sheet One)

Name.....................

DATE/S	TRAINING OBJECTIVES	METHOD USED	TIME ALLOCATED	VENUE	UNDERTAKEN BY

Model Document
P C Cripps ©

TRAINING AND DEVELOPMENT PLAN (Sheet Two)

Name....................

THE RESULTS OF THE TRAINING (QUALITATIVE AND QUANTITATIVE)	FUTURE ACTION TO BE TAKEN BY..	
	LINE MANAGER	EMPLOYEE

Model Document

Appendix 3 (*contd.*)

Name: ....
....
Date: ....

The Self Perception Inventory was created by Dr Meredith Belbin

A SELF PERCEPTION INVENTORY

DIRECTIONS

For each section distribute a total of TEN points among a maximum of three sentences which you think best describe your behaviour.

Enter the points against the appropriate letters (A to H).

1. WHAT I BELIEVE I CAN CONTRIBUTE TO A TEAM

(a) I think I can quickly see and take advantage of new opportunities.

(b) I can work well with a very wide range of people.

(c) Producing ideas is one of my natural assets.

(d) My ability rests in being able to draw people out whenever I detect they have something of value to contribute to group objectives.

(e) My capacity to follow through has much to do with my personal effectiveness.

(f) I am ready to face temporary unpopularity if it leads to worthwhile results in the end.

(g) I am quick to sense what is likely to work in a situation with which I am familiar.

(h) I can offer a reasoned case for alternative courses of action without introducing bias or prejudice.

2. IF I HAVE A POSSIBLE SHORTCOMING IN TEAM WORK, IT COULD BE THAT:

(a) I am not at ease unless meetings are well structured and controlled and generally well conducted.

(b) I am inclined to be too generous towards others who have a valid viewpoint that has not been given a proper airing.

(c) I have a tendency to talk a lot once the group gets on to new ideas.

(d) My objective outlook makes it difficult for me to join in readily and enthusiastically with colleagues.

(e) I am sometimes seen as forceful and authoritarian if there is a need to get something done.

(f) I find it difficult to lead from the front, perhaps because I am over-responsive to group atmosphere.

(g) I am apt to get too caught up in ideas that occur to me and so lose track of what is happening.

(h) My colleagues tend to see me as worrying unnecessarily over detail and the possibility that things may go wrong.

3. WHEN INVOLVED IN A PROJECT WITH OTHER PEOPLE:

(a) I have an aptitude for influencing people without pressurising them.

(b) My general vigilance prevents careless mistakes and omissions being made.

(c) I am ready to press for action to make sure that the meeting does not waste time or lose sight of the main objectives.

(d) I can be counted on to contribute something original.

(e) I am always ready to back a good suggestion in the common interest.

(f) I am keen to look for the latest in new ideas and developments.

(g) I believe my capacity for cool judgement is appreciated by others.

(h) I can be relied upon to see that all essential work is organised.

4. MY CHARACTERISTIC APPROACH TO GROUP WORK IS THAT:

(a) I have a quiet interest in getting to know colleagues better.

(b) I am not reluctant to challenge the views of others or to hold a minority view myself.

(c) I can usually find a line of argument to refute unsound propositions.

(d) I think I have a talent for making things work once a plan has to be put into operation.

(e) I have a tendency to avoid the obvious and to come out with the unexpected.

(f) I bring a touch of perfectionism to any team job I undertake.

(g) I am ready to make use of contacts outside the group itself.

(h) While I am interested in all views, I have no hesitation in making up my mind once a decision has to be made.

5. I GAIN SATISFACTION IN A JOB BECAUSE:

(a) I enjoy analysing situations and weighing up all the possible choices.

(b) I am interested in finding practical solutions to problems.

(c) I like to feel I am fostering good working relationships.

(d) I can exert a strong influence on decisions.

(e) I can meet people who may have something new to offer.

(f) I can get people to agree on a necessary course of action.

(g) I feel in my element when I can give a task my full attention.

(i) I like to find a field that stretches my imagination.

6. IF I AM SUDDENLY GIVEN A DIFFICULT TASK WITH LIMITED TIME AND UNFAMILIAR PEOPLE:

(a) I would feel like retiring to a corner to devise a way out of the impasse before developing a line.

(b) I would be ready to work with the person who showed the most positive approach however difficult he might be.

(c) I would find some way of reducing the size of task by establishing what different individuals might best contribute.

(d) My natural sense of urgency would help to ensure that we did not fall behind schedule.

(e) I believe I would keep cool and maintain my capacity to think straight.

(f) I would retain a steadiness of purpose in spite of the pressures.

(g) I would be prepared to take a positive lead if I felt the group was making no progress.

(h) I would open discussions with a view to stimulating new thoughts and getting something moving.

7. WITH REFERENCE TO THE PROBLEMS TO WHICH I AM SUBJECT TO WORKING IN GROUPS:

(a) I am apt to show my impatience with those who are obstructing progress.

(b) Others may criticise me for being too analytical and insufficiently intuitive.

(c) My desire to ensure that work is properly done can hold up proceedings.

(d) I tend to get bored rather easily and rely on one or two stimulating members to spark me off.

(e) I find it difficult to get started unless the goals are clear.

(f) I am sometimes poor at explaining and clarifying complex points that occur to me.

(g) I am conscious of demanding from others things I cannot do myself.

(h) I hesitate to get my points across when I run up against real opposition.

SELF PERCEPTION INVENTORY ANALYSIS SHEET

Transpose the scores from the points in Appendix three by entering them section by section in the table below. Then, add up the points in each column to give a total team-role distribution score.

SECTION	CW	CH	SH	PL	RI	ME	TW	CF
I	g	d	f	c	A	h	b	e
II	a	b	e	g	C	d	f	h
III	h	a	c	f	D	g	e	b
IV	d	h	b	e	G	c	a	f
V	b	f	d	h	E	a	c	g
VI	f	c	g	a	H	e	b	d
VII	e	g	e	f	D	b	h	c
TOTAL								

Appendix 4

USEFUL PEOPLE TO HAVE IN TEAMS

TYPE	SYMBOL	TYPICAL FEATURES	POSITIVE QUALITIES	ALLOWABLE WEAKNESSES
Company Worker	CW	Conservative, dutiful, predictable	Organising ability, practical common sense, hard working, self disciplined	Lack of flexibility, unresponsiveness to unproven ideas
Chairman	CH	Calm, self-confident, controlled	A capacity for treating and welcoming all potential contributors on their merits and without prejudice	No more than ordinary in terms of intellect or creative ability
Shaper	SH	Highly strung, out-going, dynamic	Drive and readiness to challenge inertia, ineffectiveness, complacency or self-deception	Prone to provocation, irritation and impatience
Plant	PL	Individualistic, serious minded, unorthodox	High IQ, imagination, knowledge	Up in the clouds, inclined to disregard practical details or protocol
Resource Investigator	RI	Extrovert, enthusiastic, curious, communicative	A capacity for contacting people and exploring anything new. An ability to respond to challenge	Liable to lose interest once the initial fascination has passed
Monitor Evaluator	ME	Sober, unemotional, prudent	Judgement, discretion, hard headedness	Lacks inspiration or the ability to motivate others
Team Worker	TW	Socially orientated, rather mild, sensitive	An ability to respond to people and to situations and to promote team spirit	Indecisiveness at moments of crisis
Completer Finisher	CF	Painstaking, orderly, conscientious, anxious	A capacity for follow through	A tendency to worry about small things. A reluctance to *"let go"*

APPENDIX 5

THE "6P" APPROACH TO BUSINESS MEETINGS

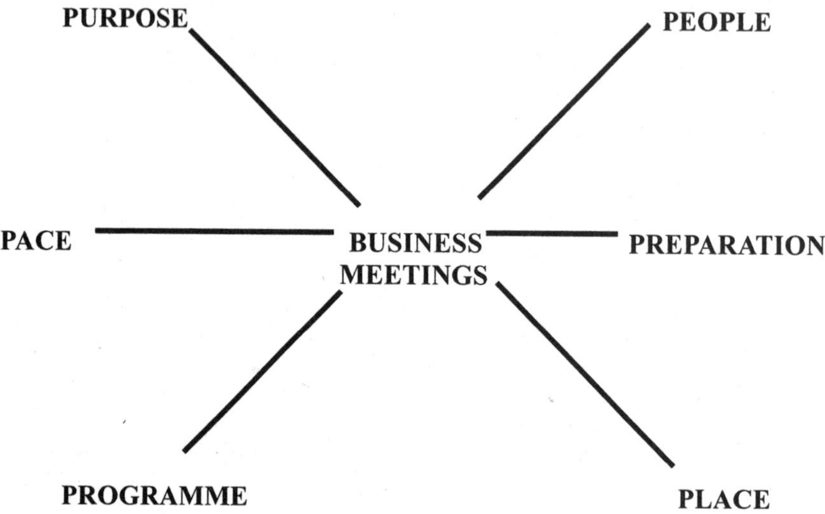

APPENDIX 6

THE PEDIGREE OF SUCCESS

A number of years ago I discovered a poem entitled *"The Pedigree of Success"*. It's one I encourage you to issue to your staff.

The father of SUCCESS is named WORK

The mother of SUCCESS is named AMBITION

The oldest son is COMMON SENSE

Some of the children are called STABILITY, PERSEVERANCE, HONESTY, THOROUGHNESS and CO-OPERATION

The baby is OPPORTUNITY

Get to know the Father and you'll be able to get along with the rest of the family.

CHECKLISTS

Checklist 1

QUANTIFIABLE TRAINING OBJECTIVES

Training is an investment in an individual or group and as such should produce a positive return. In order for that return to be measured objectives need to be set. This Checklist shows examples of QUANTIFIABLE training objectives which can be set for Field Sales personnel.

Sales Activity	Standard of Performance			% Improvement in Performance over 12 months			
	Now	6 mths	12 mths	25	50	75	100
1. Effective daily call rate on existing and prospective customers	4	5	6	→	→		
2. Number of quotations generated each week	3	4	6	→	→		
3. Number of orders secured each week	4	6	8	→	→	→	→
4. Average value of orders secured each week	15000	17500	20000	→			
5. Ratio of prospective customer calls to existing customer calls	1:5	1:3	1:25	→	→		
6. Ratio of quotations generated to total calls made	1:6	1:6	1:5	→			
7. Ratio of orders to total calls made	1:5	1:4	1:4	→			
8. Ratio of miles travelled to calls made	1:45	1:40	1:35	→			

Checklist 2

QUALITATIVE TRAINING OBJECTIVES

The effects of training cannot always be measured by numerical results. The measure has to be a QUALITATIVE one i.e. how well something is done or completed. To set qualitative objectives you have to define the BEHAVIOUR you want the individual to demonstrate.

Shown below are examples of qualitative objectives established for a supervisor who has attended a Management Development Workshop.

PERSONAL ACTION COMMITMENT	QUALITATIVE MEASUREMENT OF RESULT
1. To hold a TEAM MEETING each week	When the Supervisor is seen to have planned the meeting in line with the recommendations contained within his manual. When the Supervisor involves all members of his team in the meeting and is seen to generate enthusiasm amongst his group. When the Supervisor secures written action agreements from his team members at the conclusion of each section of the manual.
2. To conduct ON-GOING training for team members	When the Supervisor produces a formal Training Plan for each of his team members covering a period of not less than six months. When each person's Training Plan is seen to relate to individuals' strengths and shortcomings. When all training is planned in accordance with the guidelines shown within the Supervisor's Manual. When all training is seen to result in employee performance improvements.
3. To REVIEW FORMALLY each member's performance once a quarter	When the Supervisor has planned for the review discussion. When the review discussion enables the employee to give his/her assessment of the progress he/she has made during the previous quarter. When the review concludes with an agreement on the future training requirements of the team member.

CHECKLIST 3

THE QUESTIONS USED REGULARLY BY MANAGERS WHO SUCCESSFULLY DEVELOP THEIR TEAM MEMBERS

What would you do in my shoes?

How would you approach this matter?

What's your opinion?

What can we do to capitalise upon...?

How can we build upon........?

What do you consider to be the best approach?

When would you action/apply/introduce........?

When do you think action should be taken?

What benefits do you think would result from........?

What would you do if it were your money?

How could we improve upon...........?

What changes would you make to......?

Where do you think we can achieve the greatest savings?

Who do you consider to be the best person to........?

Who would you recommend for.......?

Checklist 4

ARE YOU THE BIGGEST SOURCE OF DEMOTIVATION IN YOUR DEPARTMENT, COMPANY OR ORGANISATION?

Here is a list of all too common reasons for the existence of irritation and frustration amongst employees. Which could be applied to you?

1. Failing to provide employees with recognition of their achievements.
2. Insufficient opportunities for employees to develop their knowledge and skills.
3. Inadequate healthy competition within a team.
4. Destructive competition within a team.
5. Irregular formal or informal feedback to employees on their performance.
6. A lack of genuine interest in employees.
7. Insufficient delegation.
8. A lack of leadership and direction.
9. Inconsistency of managerial behaviour.
10. A lack of management planning.
11. Managers failing to retain emotional control.
12. Managers telling people what to do without explaining why.
13. Managers' lack of natural warmth – in particular the ability or unwillingness to smile.
14. Managers always focusing upon what employees do wrong.
15. The ignoring of requests for help and guidance.
16 Irrational behaviour on the part of managers.
17 Open reprimands.
18 Breaking promises.
19 Sarcasm.
20 Unfairness.
21 The absence of managerial control.
22. Stealing credit for other peoples' ideas.

23. A failure of managers to insist on high standards of performance.
24. Favouritism.
25. Being *"two faced"*.
26. Threats – veiled or direct.
27. Managers failing to give their staff time.
28. A lack of pride.
29. Management by fear.
30. Managerial abdication of responsibility and accountability.

You may have noticed that I have made no reference to *"money"* within the Checklist. This is not because I do not recognise the importance of money to all employees. It is because I would like all managers to examine their own behaviour and its impact on employees attitudes rather than use money as the panacea for all motivational problems.

CHECKLIST 4.1

THE *"KILLER PHRASES"*

Twenty-four ways to destroy ideas and chloroform creative thinking within your team

"A good idea, but"

"We've never done it that way"

"It won't work"

"We haven't the time"

"It's not in the budget"

"We've tried that before"

"We're not ready for it yet"

"It's all right in theory"

"It's too academic"

"It's too hard to administer"

"That involves too much paperwork"

"You're too early"

"It's not good enough"

"There are better ways than that, I know"

"It's against our policy"

"Who do you think you are?"

"You haven't considered........."

"It needs more study"

"Don't be ridiculous"

"Let's be practical"

"Let me add to that"

"Let's be realistic"

"Has anyone else tried it"

"Someone would have suggested it before if it were any good"

How many of these phrases have you used within the last week with your team members?

CHECKLIST 4.2

THE *"IGNITER PHRASES"*

How to encourage ideas and develop creative thinking:

"I agree"

"That's good"

"I looked at this last night and really liked it"

"Good job"

"You're on the right track"

"That's a winner"

"That's the first time I've had anyone think of that"

"I appreciate what you have done"

"Go ahead.... try it"

"We're going to do something different today"

"I like that"

"Congratulations"

"You can do it"

"Keep up the good work"

"Fantastic"

"I'm very pleased with what you've done"

"Very good"

"Let's start a new trend"

"I made the mistake, I'm sorry"

"That's a great idea"

"That would be interesting to try"

"I couldn't do that well myself"

"I have faith in you"

"Let's make it happen"

How good an igniter are you?

Checklist 4.3

HOW WELL AM I DOING?

You cannot and should not assume you are *"managing well"*. You need feedback from your staff. Invite your team members to complete the Checklist shown below:

QUESTION	**ANSWER**
1. How effectively do I communicate to you what I expect from you?	
2. Do I talk with you or at you?	
3. Do I show sufficient interest in how you are performing your job?	
4. When I want you to adopt new techniques, processes or procedures do I always demonstrate these to you?	
5. Am I approachable?	
6. Do you feel comfortable discussing work related concerns with me?	
7. Do I listen attentively to your suggestions and recommendations?	
8. Do I treat every member of the team fairly?	
9. Do I behave in a consistent manner?	
10. What do you most wish I would do differently?	

You may consider that there is considerable risk attached to issuing the Checklist. Let me assure you that the dangers can be far greater if you live in ignorance of your team members views on your effectiveness as their manager.

CHECKLIST 5

WHAT'S DEMOTIVATING MY STAFF?

This Checklist contains many of the most common sources of demotivation amongst employees and a series of potential solutions. Maintain an awareness of your employees levels of motivation by referring to this Checklist.

CAUSE OF EMPLOYEE DEMOTIVATION	POTENTIAL SOLUTIONS
1. Lack of recognition	Regular thank you's (written and verbal) Sincere praise Bullentins/Magazines entries
2. Lack of opportunity (Do not confuse opportunity with responsibility – many people do not want increased responsibility)	Show people how to develop themselves Set projects Delegate
3. No formal performance review	Introduce quarterly reviews Link each review to an on-going Training and Development Plan
4. Weak management	Adopt a firm but fair approach
5. Management by Directive	Involve people in decision making
6. A *"Telling and not Selling"* Management style	Substitute questions for statements
7. A superficial interest in people	Speak to each team member about his/her interests rather than his/her job
8. Open reprimands	Exercise self control – always correct individuals in private
9. *"Playing Politics"*	Don't
10. Breaking promises	Keep each promise
11. Sarcasm	When in doubt, leave humour out

CAUSE OF EMPLOYEE DEMOTIVATION	POTENTIAL SOLUTIONS
12. Threats – veiled or direct	Never threaten
13. Stealing credit for someone else's idea	Give credit openly
14. Ignoring or discouraging suggestions	Encourage suggestions – adopt my R.O.I approach. R.O.I means Return On Involvement
15. Allowing atmospheres to develop	Work at creating a team – do not settle for managing a group of individuals
16. Favouritism	Treat everyone equally
17. Too little work Too little supervision Too little measurement	Set your standards – make them stretching but realistic
18. Lack of management consistency	Ensure that all your actions are consistent (and this does not mean being predictable)
19. An unwillingness to listen to others	Become an active listener by seeking peoples' ideas and views
20. A lack of management planning	The starting point for **all** management activity is planning

Checklist 6

HOW CAN YOU ASSESS HOW WELL YOU PLAN, ORGANISE AND CONDUCT YOUR MEETINGS?

The purpose of this Checklist is to allow you to assess your own effectiveness in the important skill of running meetings.

Ask yourself the following questions:

1. Do I always make staff feel at home in the meeting environment?
2. Are the training room arrangements always as satisfactory as I could economically make them?
3. Do I always start on time?
4. Do I always finish on or before the time stated?
5. Do I ever hold a meeting without having set clear objectives?
6. Do I ever make participants look small by airing my superior knowledge?
7. Do I ever criticise a question destructively?
8. Do I always generate the maximum amount of constructive participation?
9. Do I ever seat my staff facing an open window? (A constant source of distraction)
10. Do I always ensure my visual aids are visible to everybody in the room?
11. Do I always ensure every member of the team participates?
12. Am I certain that everybody always hears and understands what I say?
13. Do I always state the objective(s) clearly at the beginning of each meeting?
14. Am I always enthusiastic at a meeting?
15. Am I ever insincere?
16. After each meeting do I always try and assess its effectiveness?
17. Do my team find the meetings I hold valuable?
18. Do I always uphold my company's policies and decisions?

19. Do I always give adequate notice of meetings?
20. Do I ever use profane or offensive language when talking to a group?
21. Do I always try to control any bad personal mannerisms which could reduce the effectiveness of my contributions to meetings?
22. Although pleasant, am I always firm at meetings?
23. Am I continually aware of the group's reactions?
24. Do I ever try to put over too many subjects in too short a time?
25. Am I ever afraid to point out the obvious?
26. Do I always summarise clearly and logically?
27. Do I think I am perfect at holding meetings?
28. Is my planning always thorough?
29. Do I search for and consider new methods of training?
30. Do I ever allow a meeting to become an end in itself?
31. Do I always try and foresee possible personality problems?
32. Do I realise that many of my opinions are firmly based on prejudice?

Keep this – and re-appraise and rate yourself every six months.

Checklist 7

A MANAGER'S GUIDE TO TRAINING METHODS (Sheet One)

METHOD	WHAT IT IS	WHAT IT DOES	POINTS TO WATCH
1. Distance Learning	An employee is given material to study (written, audio or cd) and to comment upon.	For self-motivated individuals it can be an effective means of transferring information and prompting discussion.	Individuals need to be enthused and need to work to clear guidelines. If they are simply asked to study the material then managers can make the assumption that the individual understands, accepts and agrees with what he/she has studied.
2. Lecture	A talk with little or no audience participation.	It provides a means of transferring information to a large audience with controlled content and timing.	The lack of audience participation is likely to prevent some people understanding or assimilating the information conveyed. It is essential to avoid the presentation of too much information.

A MANAGER'S GUIDE TO TRAINING METHODS (Sheet Two)

METHOD	WHAT IT IS	WHAT IT DOES	POINTS TO WATCH
3. Interactive Discussions	The manager leads discussion on a particular topic and encourages audience involvement.	It is particularly useful when attitudes need to be influenced as a pre-cursor to knowledge transfer.	Participation encourages learning and interest. However, all the group may not join in. The discussion may also become protracted and destructive. Firm leadership is necessary.
4. Demonstration	The manager shows team members HOW to do something.	It conveys to the audience or individual that theory and practice can and should be the same thing.	The manager needs to be sure he or she is competent when demonstrating the skill, otherwise the credibility of both will be undermined.
5. Role-Play	Trainees are required to practise the skills to which they have been introduced.	Role plays enable individuals to practise skills in situations which relate to their jobs and to receive feedback from the trainer and other observers.	Role plays create emotional pressure and can lead to individuals being embarrassed. Participants should be advised that without practise and analysis they will be unable to identify their strengths and eliminate, or at least reduce the effects of, their shortcomings.

A MANAGER'S GUIDE TO TRAINING METHODS (Sheet Three)

METHOD	WHAT IT IS	WHAT IT DOES	POINTS TO WATCH
6. Quiz Sessions	A structured question and answer session which can be conducted on a one to one basis or with a group of employees who compete in teams against one another.	It can provide a light hearted means of testing individuals' retention and understanding of information.	Questions have to be skilfully constructed. When a team quiz is conducted the manager needs to be seen to be fair when fulfilling the role of chairman.
7. Case Study	A description of a real event or situation which contains details facts, figures and supporting information.	It tests individuals' or groups' ability to analyse detailed and often complicated situations and circumstances, and to determine solutions.	If the case study cannot be seen by employees to relate to their roles and responsibilities it may be considered academic in nature and of little practical value.
8. Project	An assignment with wide guidelines and one which may be undertaken over a lengthy period of time.	It should encourage individuals to show initiative and creativity. It should also stimulate individuals decision-making skills.	Trainees must be willing recipients of projects, since they can be very time consuming. Managers need to show an active interest in their team members' progress with their projects.

CHECKLIST 7.1

THE TRAINING CYCLE

1. EXPLANATION
What the task is

4. EXAMINATION
Correct and Consolidate

2. DEMONSTRATION
How the task is to be done

3. APPLICATION
Let the trainee try

As a Trainer and Developer, it is also important to bear in mind that people learn best by **DOING**, and therefore, the balance of time will be placed upon the **APPLICATION** part of the Training Cycle.

Evidence of effective training over the years, has indicated the following balance to be a reasonable aim when training.

EXPLANATION	10% of time
DEMONSTRATION	25% of time
APPLICATION }	65% of time
EXAMINATION }	

CHECKLIST 8

HOW CAN YOU EVALUATE WHETHER YOU ARE DELEGATING EFFECTIVELY?

Ask yourself these questions and place a tick in the appropriate box if your answer is *"yes"* (even if your *"yes"* is a qualified one).

1. Have I ever deferred or cancelled holidays or days off because of my workload? ☐
2. Do I feel overworked on frequent occasions? ☐
3. Have I a tendency to leave jobs unfinished? ☐
4. Do I take work home frequently? ☐
5. Do I always seem to have too much work to do? ☐
6. Do I often find myself too busy to plan future activities? ☐
7. Do my recreation activities often get cancelled? ☐
8. Have I developed a reputation as a *"problem solver"*? ☐
9. Do I have trouble meeting those deadlines set for me? ☐
10. Do I regard myself as a perfectionist? ☐
11. Am I inclined to disregard or discourage opinions from my team members? ☐
12. Am I regarded within the company as a person who issues orders? ☐
13. Do I often consider that my team members are reluctant to make their own decisions? ☐
14. Do I often consider that my team members lack initiative? ☐
15. Do my team members often come to me for advice and support? ☐
16. Do I think I have too many *"I'll do just enough"* people in my team? ☐
17. Do I consider that my team members' skills have not developed over the last twelve months? ☐
18. Do I have a team who rarely bring me new ideas or new ways of doing their jobs? ☐

Review each of these questions at least twice each year.

CHECKLIST 9

PERFORMANCE REVIEWS

Prior to conducting your next review of the performance of one of your team members ask yourself the following questions:

1. What do I consider to be my team member's major STRENGTHS?
2. How can I encourage him or her to develop them still further or use them more often?
3. What do I consider to be my team member's most significant SHORT-COMINGS?
4. How can I show him or her how to eliminate these shortcomings, or at least, reduce their effects?
5. What ATTITUDINAL changes do I want my team member to make in the next three months?
6. What additional KNOWLEDGE do I want him or her to acquire during the next three months?
7. What new SKILLS do I want him or her to acquire during the next three months?
8. What existing SKILLS do I want him or her to develop during the next quarter?
9. How confident am I that I can demonstrate the skills I want him or her to acquire?
10. How confident am I that I can show my team member how to develop his or her existing skills?

Checklist 10

HOW TO CREATE A *"SUCCESS CULTURE"* WITHIN YOUR TEAM

By developing the confidence and competence of the people who work with and for you, you increase your company's likelihood of success.

Success can be defined in a variety of ways. However, regardless of the criteria used it is important to generate a *"success culture"* within your organisation. Achieving that goal can be helped by issuing each of your staff with the Checklist shown below.

SUCCESS IS ABOUT:

1. PERSEVERANCE – as Thomas Edison said *"Genius is 1% inspiration and 99% perspiration."*
2. ACTION – make don't wait for things to happen.
3. TRYING THE UNTRIED – let's challenge the status quo – let's think the unthinkable.
4. DOING WHAT OTHERS SAY CAN'T BE DONE – success comes in cans and not can'ts.
5. ELIMINATING NEGATIVES – negative thoughts, words, phrases, body language and correspondence.
6. HAVING HIGH EXPECTATIONS – shoot for the stars.
7. ACCEPTING OWNERSHIP – play your part as a team member.
8. ACCEPTING RESPONSIBILITY – don't walk away from obstacles, see them as opportunities.
9. ACCEPTING ACCOUNTABILITY – accept criticism as well as praise.
10. ACHIEVING CONSISTENCY – success is transient unless you do the right things consistently.

CHECKLIST 11

HOW WELL DO YOU COMMUNICATE VERBALLY WITH YOUR STAFF?

Make a habit of asking yourself the following questions every three or four months:

1. Do I always consider the attitude of my team members towards the subject I wish to present?
2. Do I always seek to present my ideas in a manner that acknowledges (in a positive way) individuals' attitudes?
3. Do I always ensure that I communicate in a manner which is appropriate to my team member's level of knowledge of my subject?
4. Do I always seek to present my ideas, suggestions and recommendations in a manner that shows I am tuned in to my team member's favourite radio station – W.I.I.F.M (What's In It For Me)?
5. Do I always consider the timing of my communication with my staff?
6. Do I always consider the location of my communication with my staff?
7. Am I always clear about the objective I want to achieve from my communication?
8. Do I always rehearse my proposed approach to communicating emotionally sensitive issues?
9. Do I always consider whether my verbal communication would be complemented by visual aids?
10. Do I always ensure my communication style is "you", "we" and "us" orientated, rather than "me", "my" and "I"?
11. Do I always check my team member's understanding and acceptance of, and willingness to action, my communication?
12. Do I always seek to convey my communication without padding, bluffing, pontification, cliches or platitudes?
13. Do I always consider where verbal emphasis should or should not be put in my communication?
14. Do I always seek to talk with rather than at my team members?
15. Do I always listen to (rather than just hear) my team members responses to my communication?

16. Do I always consider the pace of my communication?
17. Do I always ensure my communication with my staff is directed towards informing rather than performing?
18. Do I always use a passive questioning technique when I want to establish the real attitudes of my staff towards a particular subject?
19. Do I always convey new ideas in a positive manner?
20. Do I always use questions to stimulate communication with my staff rather than express statements?

Checklist 12

INTERACTIVE GROUP PRESENTATIONS – ASSESSMENT CHECKLIST

When you use ROLE-PLAYS to train and develop the formal presentation skills of your staff invite other members of your team to assess the confidence and competence of their colleague by using the Checklist shown below.

Each section should be assessed by using my FORCED CHOICE RATING SYSTEM (2-4-6-8) where

2 = Below acceptable standard

4 = Acceptable standard

6 = Above acceptable standard

8 = Exceptional performance

Assessment Area	Rating	What should be Assessed?
1. SUBJECT MATTER		How well did the presenter know his/her subject?
2. VOICE PROJECTION		Was the presenter clear and understandable? Did he/she vary his/her tone? Did he/she vary his/her pace?
3. ENTHUSIASM		Was the subject presented with genuine enthusiasm?
4. SINCERITY		Did the presenter believe in what he/she was saying? Was this apparent?
5. AUDIENCE PARTICIPATION		Was the presenter interactive in style? Did all members of the audience have an opportunity to become involved?
6. QUESTIONING		Did the presenter seek to check his/her audience's understanding and acceptance of what he/she put forward?

Assessment Area	Rating	What should be Assessed?
7. SEQUENCE		Was the subject matter presented in a sequence which the audience could follow? Was the AIDA formula applied by the presenter?
8. SUMMARY		Did the presenter conclude his/her presentation with a clear and concise summary?
TOTAL RATING		

CHECKLIST 13

PERSUASIVE COMMUNICATION ROLE-PLAY – ASSESSMENT CHECKLIST

When you conduct ROLE-PLAYS in group training sessions, to develop the persuasive communication skills of your sales personnel invite other members of your team to assess the competence of their colleague by using the Checklist shown below:

ASSESSMENT AREA	TICK ENTRY			
	2	4	6	8
1. OPENING THE APPOINTMENT/MEETING (Gaining attention – scene setting, establishing a direction for the discussion)				
2. STRUCTURED QUESTIONING (The identification of the potential buyer's wants, interests, needs and expectations)				
3. CONFIRMING THE BUYER'S REQUIREMENTS (Summarising the requirements identified through structured questioning)				
4. PRESENTATION OF IDEAS/PROPOSALS/ CONCEPTS (How well were the ideas put across – were they expressed in terms of benefits to the buyer?)				
5. VISUAL AIDS (How well were visual aids used to reinforce the verbal presentations of proposals/ideas?)				
6. OBJECTION HANDLING (Were the real objections identified from amongst the excuses, stalling devices and reservations? Were the real objections handled by means of the Accept – Agree – Capitalise technique?)				

ASSESSMENT AREA	TICK ENTRY			
	2	4	6	8
7. LISTENING SKILLS (Did the persuader listen actively? Were vital verbal signals missed?)				
8. BODY LANGUAGE (Did the persuader recognise and respond to his/her contact's body language?)				
9. EMPATHY (How well did the persuader seek to understand his/her contact's attitudes and circumstances?)				
10. MENTAL AGILITY (How quick was the persuader to react to issues raised by his/her contact?)				
11. VERBAL DEXTERITY (How well did the persuader use varied language to convey his/her points?)				
12. ACTION AGREEMENT SIGNALS (Did the persuader recognise his/her contact's willingness to accept the proposals/ideas put forward? Did the persuader act upon the signals?)				
13. ACTION AGREEMENTS (Were action agreements reached? Were they the right ones? Were they secured at the earliest opportunity?)				
TOTALS				

Rating System:
2 = Below acceptable standard
4 = Acceptable standard
6 = Above acceptable standard
8 = Exceptional performance

CHECKLIST 14

DO YOU SEEK TO INCREASE YOUR TEAM MEMBERS' *"JOB SATISFACTION"*?

Individuals only develop and grow when they are engaged in activities they WANT to do. Providing job satisfaction is one of a manager's most important activities. Use the checklist below to determine if you are providing your team members with job satisfaction:

1. Do I show a regular and sustained interest in each of my employees' performances?
2. Do I provide recognition for my team members achievements?
3. Do I seek to provide my team members with a sense of security at work?
4. Do I stimulate team members interest in our products and services?
5. Do I encourage team work amongst employees?
6. Do I stimulate an atmosphere of mutual respect among team members?
7. Do I seek to provide individuals with opportunities to grow within their job?
8. Do I encourage individuals to seek greater responsibility?
9. Do I seek to place team members in jobs for which they are attitudinally and aptitudinally suited?
10. Do I provide firm but fair supervision?
11. Do I behave consistently towards my team members?
12. Do I seek to ensure my team members are remunerated above the market norm?

Review this checklist every three/four months.

Checklist 15

HAVE YOU THE RIGHT LEADERSHIP QUALITIES?

As I have already stated earlier in this book leadership is not a precise practice. However, successful leaders in business do display a number of shared qualities. How many of these qualities do you demonstrate? Find out by answering the following questions:

1. Am I seen by my team members to be visionary?
2. Do I demonstrate on a consistent basis self-confidence?
3. Do I demonstrate confidence in the people who work for and with me?
4. Do I set high performance standards for myself?
5. Do I set high performance standards for my team members?
6. Am I decisive?
7. Do I act promptly on my decisions?
8. Do I challenge the status quo?
9. Am I always looking for ways to do things better?
10. Am I prepared to experiment with change?
11. Do I encourage my team members to act on their own accord?
12. Do I lead from the front?
13. Do I encourage staff to work as a team rather than as individuals?
14. Do I recognise team members contributions?
15. Do I behave in a consistent manner?

To how many of these questions did you reply "YES"?